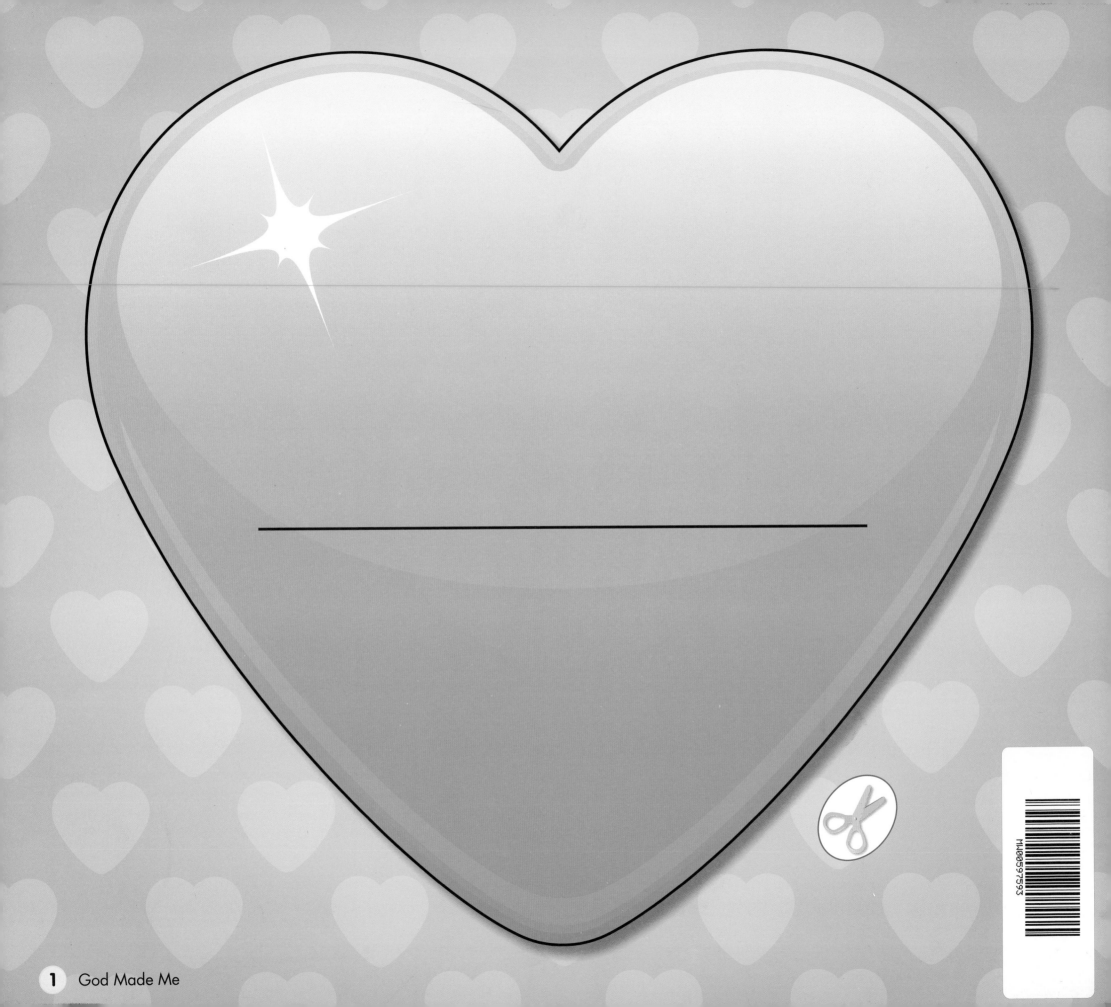

I'm special!

© LOYOLAPRESS.

Name _____

Color the ears under things you can hear.

Family Time

Chapter 1: I Can Hear

Each lesson in *God Made Me* is about a marvelous power God gives us. In this first lesson the children reflected on the gift of hearing and things they can hear, including their name. They found out that in school they will hear about God and Jesus. They heard that the Bible is a book in which God speaks to them.

Your Child

Three-year-olds are becoming more aware of themselves. Share with your child how you chose his or her name. As your child builds self-esteem by using the powers God gave him or her, encourage your child to try new things. When speaking to your child, use attention-grabbing words, such as *new*, *different*, *surprise*, or *secret* to keep him or her listening. When your child speaks, listen with full attention and look at him or her. Your child will then learn this skill.

Reflect

"Jesus is my Son whom I love. Listen to him." (adapted from Matthew 17:5)

Pray

Father, help us to hear and obey your Word.

Do

• Go for a walk with your child and listen for sounds of nature.
• Fill glasses with varying levels of water and have your child tap the sides with a spoon.
• Use modeling clay to form your child's initial.
• Use your child's name in songs.
• Read to your child *The Listening Walk* by Paul Showers. After a moment of quiet, encourage your child to identify sounds he or she heard. Thank God for giving us ears and good things to hear.

For more family resources, refer to the Family Activity Booklet and visit www.loyolapress.com/preschool.

© LOYOLAPRESS.

Name _____

Write an **X** in each circle.

Family Time

Chapter 2: I Can See

In this lesson the children studied the precious gift of vision that God gave them. They talked about how their eyes help them and named things they like to see. They made a beautiful picture in class to give joy to anyone who sees it. Ask your child to tell you the Bible story about the woman who used her eyes to find her coin (Luke 15:8–10). Comment that God values us and keeps us in sight.

Your Child

Our vision is a source of delight. Call your child's attention to lovely sights (a flower, a sunrise, a field, clouds) and make it a practice to thank God for what you see as well as the ability to see.

Reflect

My eyes are upon you, O God, my Lord[.] (Psalm 141:8)

Pray

God, open our eyes to the beauty of your creation.

Do

- Point out various shapes to your child.
- Teach your child the names of colors. Finish a meal with a colorful dessert, such as rainbow sherbet or layered gelatin.
- Look out a window with your child, especially when it is raining or snowing.
- Let your child use a magnifying glass or binoculars.
- Display your child's work.
- Take your child to the zoo or to a garden to see God's creations.
- Read to your child *Can You See What I See?* by Walter Wick. Talk about the pictures to guide his or her appreciation of the gift of sight. Thank God for giving us eyes and beautiful things to see.

For more family resources, refer to the Family Activity Booklet and visit **www.loyolapress.com/preschool.**

© LOYOLAPRESS.

Name _____

Circle the things that smell good.

Chapter 3: I Can Smell

In this lesson the children reflected on their sense of smell. They practiced identifying various aromas. They heard the story of the woman who gave Jesus the gift of perfume (Mark 14:3–9), and they learned about the use of incense in church. Admire your child's picture of flowers made in class. Ask your child to sing for you the song that begins "I've a nose," sung to the tune of "Mary Had a Little Lamb."

Your Child

Lead your child to appreciate our sense of smell by pointing out the aromas of certain foods cooking, flowers, and just-cut grass. Make your child aware of the smell of certain places: a barn, a bakery, a library, a beach.

Reflect

For we are the aroma of Christ for God among those who are being saved . . . (2 Corinthians 2:15)

Pray

Holy Spirit, help us to be the aroma of Christ in the world.

Do

- Let your child put on cologne and then enjoy the fragrance together.
- With your child, plan a meal of foods that smell especially good.
- Have your child close his or her eyes and identify certain foods that have distinctive smells: toast, orange slices, pizza, strawberries, popcorn.
- Visit a garden with your child and smell the flowers.
- Read to your child *Little Bunny Follows His Nose* by Katherine Howard. Ask your child to name other things they like to smell. Thank God for our sense of smell.

For more family resources, refer to the Family Activity Booklet and visit **www.loyolapress.com/preschool.**

© LOYOLA PRESS.

God Made Me

Name

God Made Me

© LOYOLAPRESS.

Name_____

Color the boxes red under the hot things.

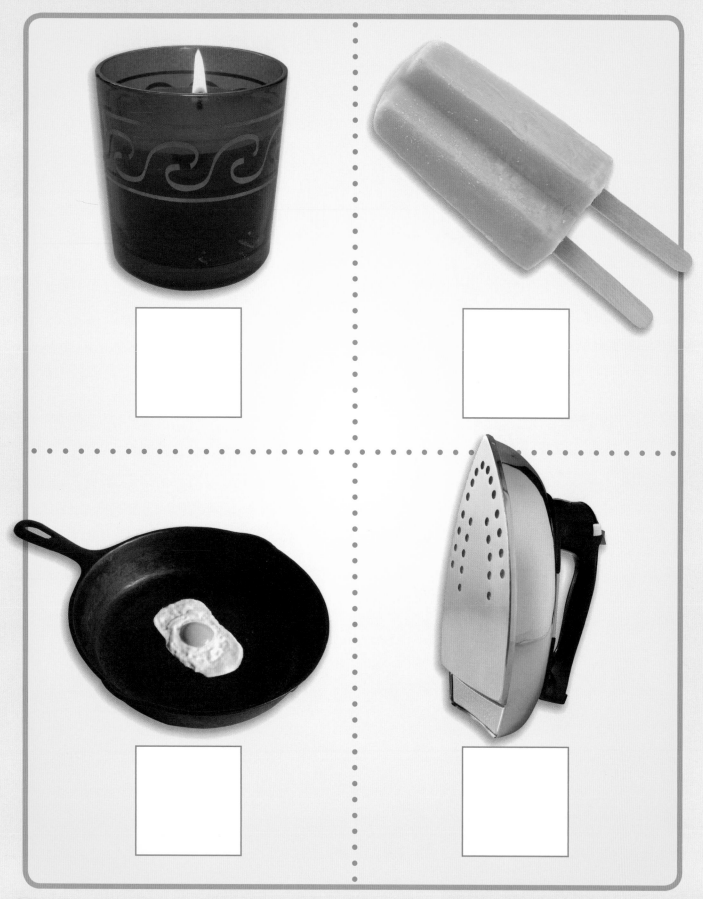

Chapter 4: I Can Touch

In this lesson the children focused on their sense of touch. They played with clay or play dough and identified the way objects in the room felt. They also made collages from material with various textures. Ask your child to tell you how pieces of his or her collage feel.

Your Child

Our actions communicate our love. Your child needs to be assured frequently of your love by signs such as holding, cuddling, snuggling, back-rubbing, tickling, hand-holding, squeezing, and hugs and kisses.

Reflect

At sunset all who had people sick with various diseases brought them to [Jesus]. He laid his hands on each of them and cured them. (Luke 4:40)

Pray

Jesus, may we know your healing presence in our lives.

Do

• Let your child help make cookies by mixing dough, forming shapes, or using a cookie cutter.
• Provide clay, play dough, or a sandbox for your child.
• Call attention to things in nature that feel good: the sun's rays, a breeze on a hot day, grass under bare feet, or mud squishing between toes.
• Make your child "goop" to squeeze and hold: Mix three tablespoons of cornstarch and two tablespoons of cold water.
• Read to your child *My Hands* by Aliki. Ask your child to name five things we can do with our hands. Thank God for hands and the gift of touch.

For more family resources, refer to the Family Activity Booklet and visit **www.loyolapress.com/preschool.**

© LOYOLAPRESS.

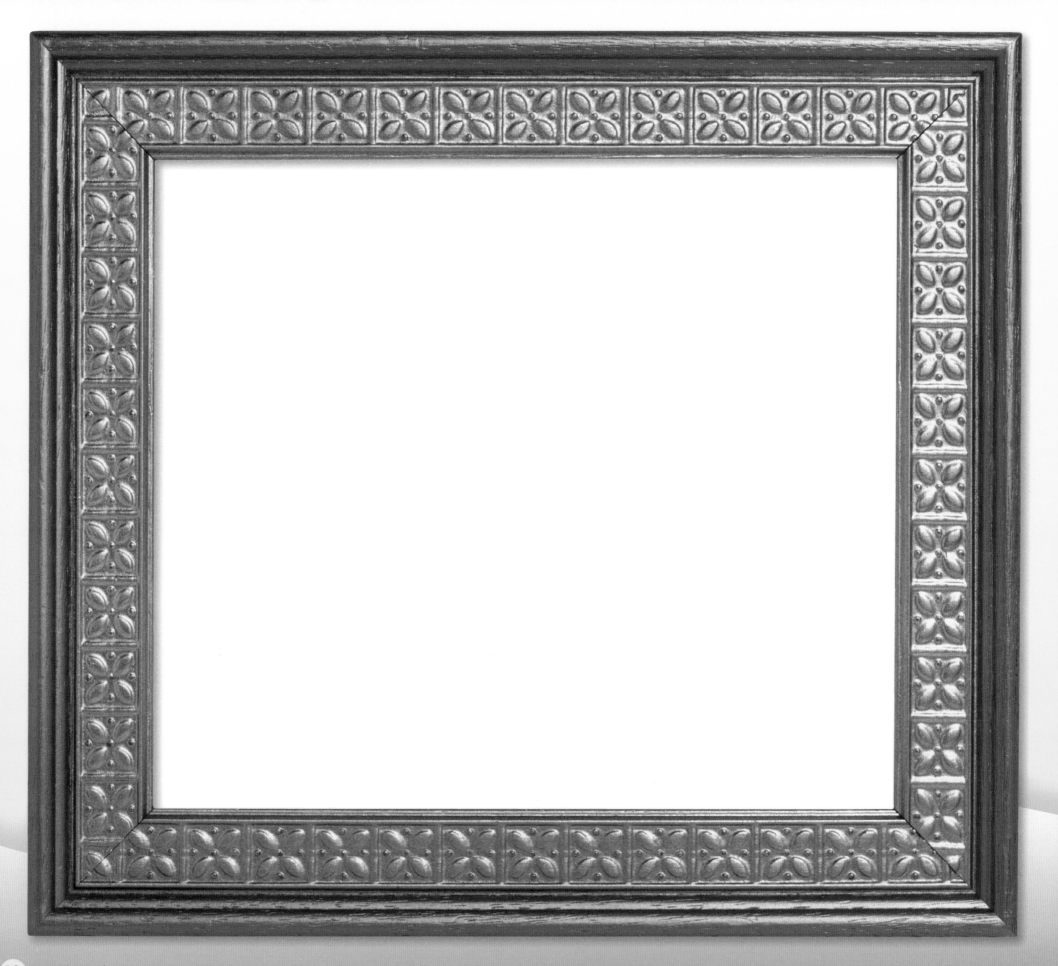

Name _____

© LOYOLA PRESS.

Name_____

Circle foods that grow on trees.

Family Time

Chapter 5: I Can Taste

In this lesson the children learned about their sense of taste. They talked about their favorite food and were encouraged to eat a variety of foods. As a culmination of their study of the five senses, they had a party to celebrate themselves. Ask your child to show you the right order of the four pictures of a pizza.

Your Child

Children need a balanced diet. Keep snacks as healthful as possible and limit sugar, fat, and salt in your child's diet. Children have food preferences. You need not insist that your child eat foods that he or she strongly dislikes. You might serve your child's favorite meal sometime this week. Begin this meal with a short prayer of thanks to God.

Reflect

Learn to savor how good the LORD is[.]
(Psalm 34:9)

Pray

Loving God, we praise you for your goodness and love.

Do

- Let your child go with you when you shop for food.
- Visit a farm and talk about the food it produces. Comment how good and wise God was in planning our food.
- Take your child to an ice-cream store and let him or her choose a flavor for a cone.
- Once in a while serve a new food to your child.
- Read to your child *Bread and Jam for Frances* by Russell Hoban. Discuss why it is nice to try and enjoy a variety of tastes. Thank God for the sense of taste and for good foods to eat.

For more family resources, refer to the Family Activity Booklet and visit **www.loyolapress.com/preschool.**

© LOYOLAPRESS.

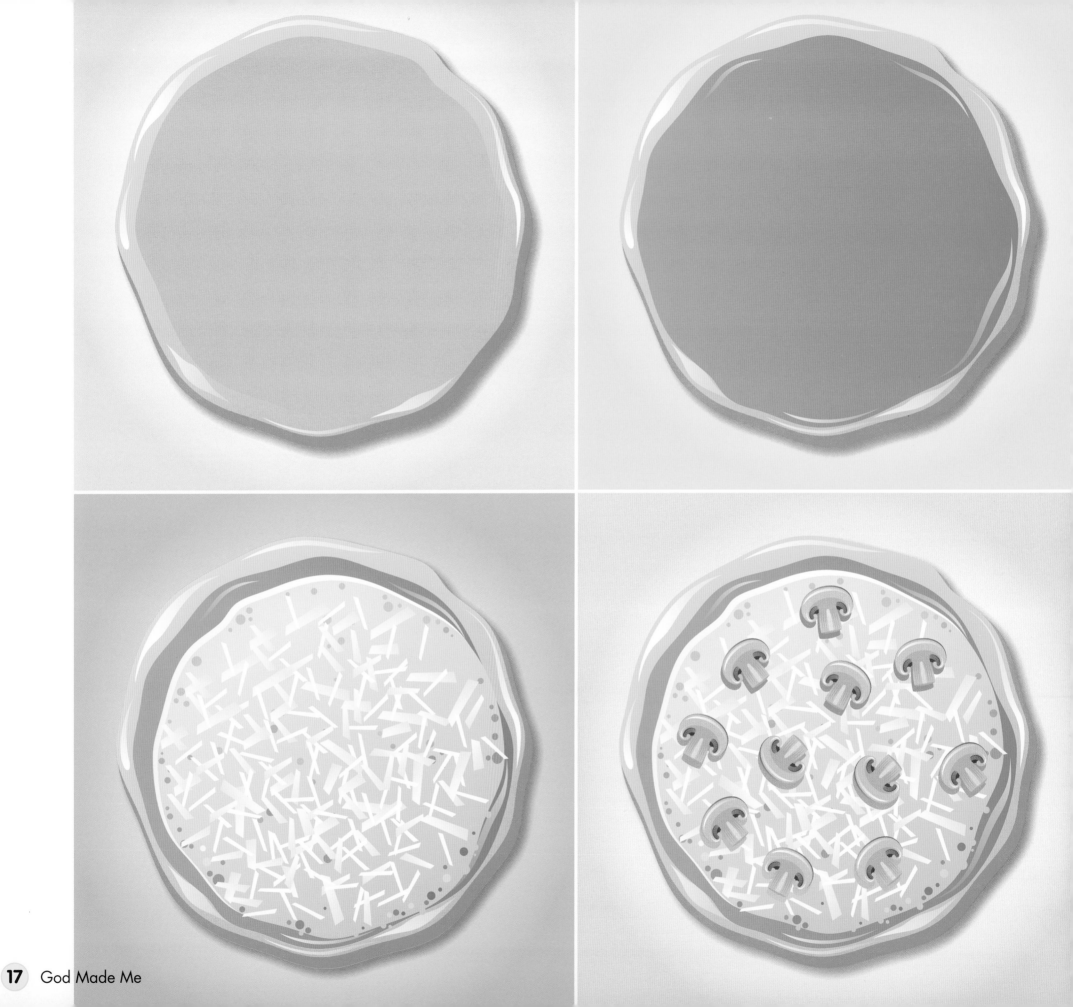

© LOYOLAPRESS.

Have someone trace your shoe for you.
Make a picture of your shoe.

Chapter 6: I Can Help

In this lesson the children talked about helping. They heard that Jesus helped people, and they learned how they can help. They made a picture of their shoe to remind them that they can run to help. Your child was awarded a medal for being a helper. When he or she helps you, affix a star to the medal or draw one on it. Look at the story together and ask your child to tell you about Bobby.

Your Child

A Christian serves others as Christ served. Even young children can be real helpers at home. Helping gives them a sense of being needed and a feeling of belonging. Ask for your child's assistance, praise his or her efforts, and thank him or her. You will cultivate the habit of ministering to others and develop responsibility in your child.

Reflect

Two men who were blind cried out to Jesus, "Lord, have pity on us!" Jesus stopped and asked, "What do you want me to do for you?" They said, "We want to see." Jesus touched their eyes and immediately they received their sight and followed him. (adapted from Matthew 20:30–34)

Pray

Lord, help us follow your example of loving service.

Do

- Let your child help set the table, prepare a meal, carry packages, feed the pet, entertain a younger sibling, or help with yard work.
- Talk about people who help the community.
- Read to your child *Herman the Helper* by Robert Kraus. Name ways your child helps others. Thank God for opportunities to help.

For more family resources, refer to the Family Activity Booklet and visit **www.loyolapress.com/preschool.**

© LOYOLAPRESS.

That night Mom and Dad give Bobby a hug and a present—and it isn't even his birthday. The present says, "I'm a super helper!"

4

Bobby the Helper

At breakfast Bobby helps butter the toast.

1

Name_____

Later he helps Mom with shopping . . .

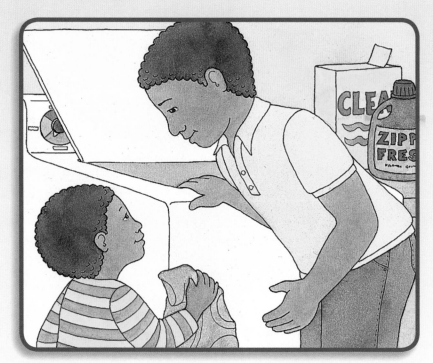

and Dad with the laundry.

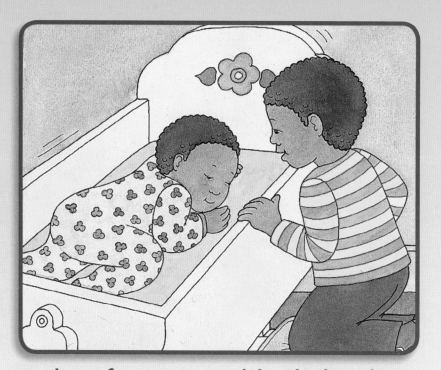

In the afternoon Bobby helps the baby go to sleep.

Then he helps wash the car.

2

3

© LOYOLA PRESS.

© LOYOLA PRESS.

Name _____

Color the hearts by things that have been cared for.

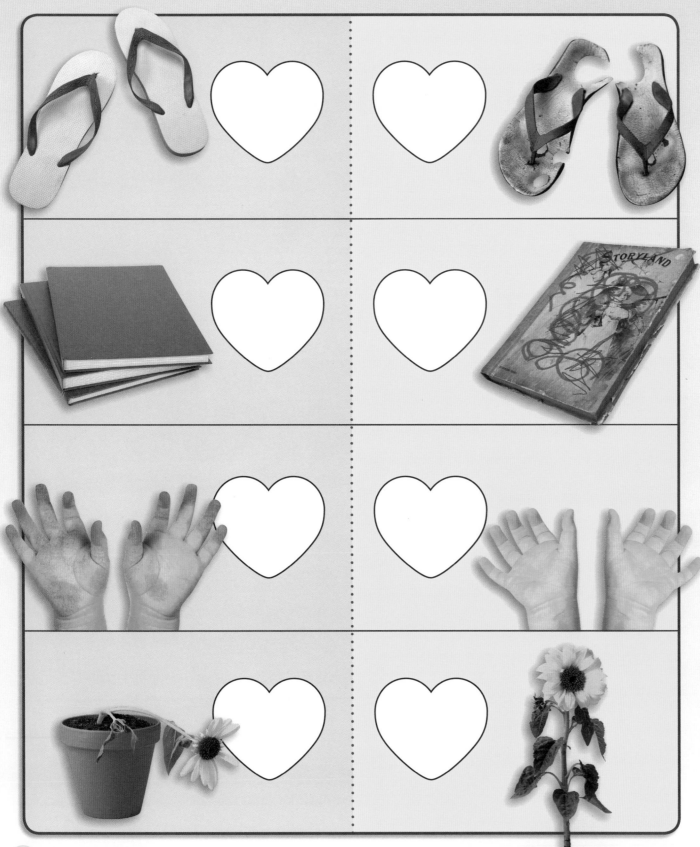

Chapter 7: I Can Care

In this lesson the children learned that God expects us to care for the gifts of this world. They talked about ways to care for grass and flowers, animals, their own things, and themselves. Ask your child what the jack-in-the-box made in class helps him or her remember (to care for things and themselves).

Your Child

Continue to train your child to practice healthful habits, such as eating good foods, brushing teeth regularly, washing hands, and dressing for the weather. Three-and-a-half-year-old children may balk at routines. During this phase, someone other than the primary caregiver may have more success with the child at mealtimes or when the child is getting dressed.

Reflect

God gives the earth rain. God makes grass grow. God gives food to birds and other animals. (adapted from Psalm 104:13–14)

Pray

God, help us to care for the earth and all of creation.

Do

• Teach your child not to run water unnecessarily.
• Let your child help plant or water flowers.
• Give your child a special responsibility at home: caring for a plant, dusting a table, straightening the newspapers.
• Read a bedtime story to your child to entice him or her to go to bed on time.
• Read to your child *Harry the Dirty Dog* by Gene Zion. Discuss ways we care for ourselves and others. Thank God for his love and care.

For more family resources, refer to the Family Activity Booklet and visit **www.loyolapress.com/preschool.**

© LOYOLAPRESS.

Name_____

Draw lines to connect things that are used together to clean.

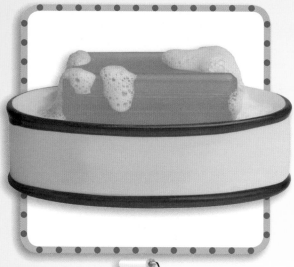

Family Time

Chapter 8: I Can Clean

In this lesson the children talked about keeping things and themselves clean. They told how they helped clean at home and learned that washing their hands is important. They played with water and thanked God for this creation that enables us to clean. Have your child work the puzzle made in class.

Your Child

Preschoolers are capable of learning how to clean. In fact they enjoy cleaning things. Make use of this characteristic to occupy your child, provide exercise, and take care of small chores.

Reflect

I will sprinkle clean water to cleanse you. (adapted from Ezekiel 36:25)

Pray

Merciful God, cleanse us from sin and make us holy.

Do

- Make bath time an even happier experience by providing toys, bath crayons, sponges cut in shapes, and colorful scented soap.
- Let your child do small tasks as you clean your house, yard, garage, or car.
- With your child, watch cleaners at work: street cleaners, window cleaners, people at a car wash.
- Go for a walk in the rain with your child.
- Teach your child to put away his or her toys and clothes.
- Read to your child *How Do Dinosaurs Clean Their Rooms?* by Jane Yolen. Discuss how your child can pick up toys and other belongings. Thank God for all the ways we keep ourselves clean and respect our belongings.

For more family resources, refer to the Family Activity Booklet and visit **www.loyolapress.com/preschool.**

© LOYOLAPRESS.

Name _____

Color the bread and pitcher.

Family Time

Chapter 9: I Can Share

In this lesson the children heard that God wants us to share the gifts of the earth with others because we are all brothers and sisters in God's family. They learned that sharing brings joy to the giver and the receiver. Comment on the picture your child made by "sharing" paint on one side of the paper with the other side.

Your Child

For children, sharing is difficult and hard to understand. They consider their things a part of them, so when they keep favorite items for themselves, they are not merely being selfish. Look for opportunities to encourage your child to share food, toys, and books. Make your child aware of how you share. Christian love is taught most effectively in the home.

Reflect

If someone is hungry, share your food. If someone is thirsty, share your drink. If someone has no clothes, share your clothes. (adapted from Matthew 25:35–36)

Pray

Gracious God, help us to share generously with others.

Do

- Teach your child to take turns, and praise your child whenever he or she shares something.
- Give your child a present, such as crayons and a coloring book, to share.
- Donate food, toys, or clothes to a shelter for people who are homeless. Make your child aware of your sharing and the satisfaction it gives you.
- Read to your child *The Rainbow Fish* by Marcus Pfister. Name times your child has shared with others. Thank God for the joy of sharing.

For more family resources, refer to the Family Activity Booklet and visit **www.loyolapress.com/preschool.**

© LOYOLA PRESS.

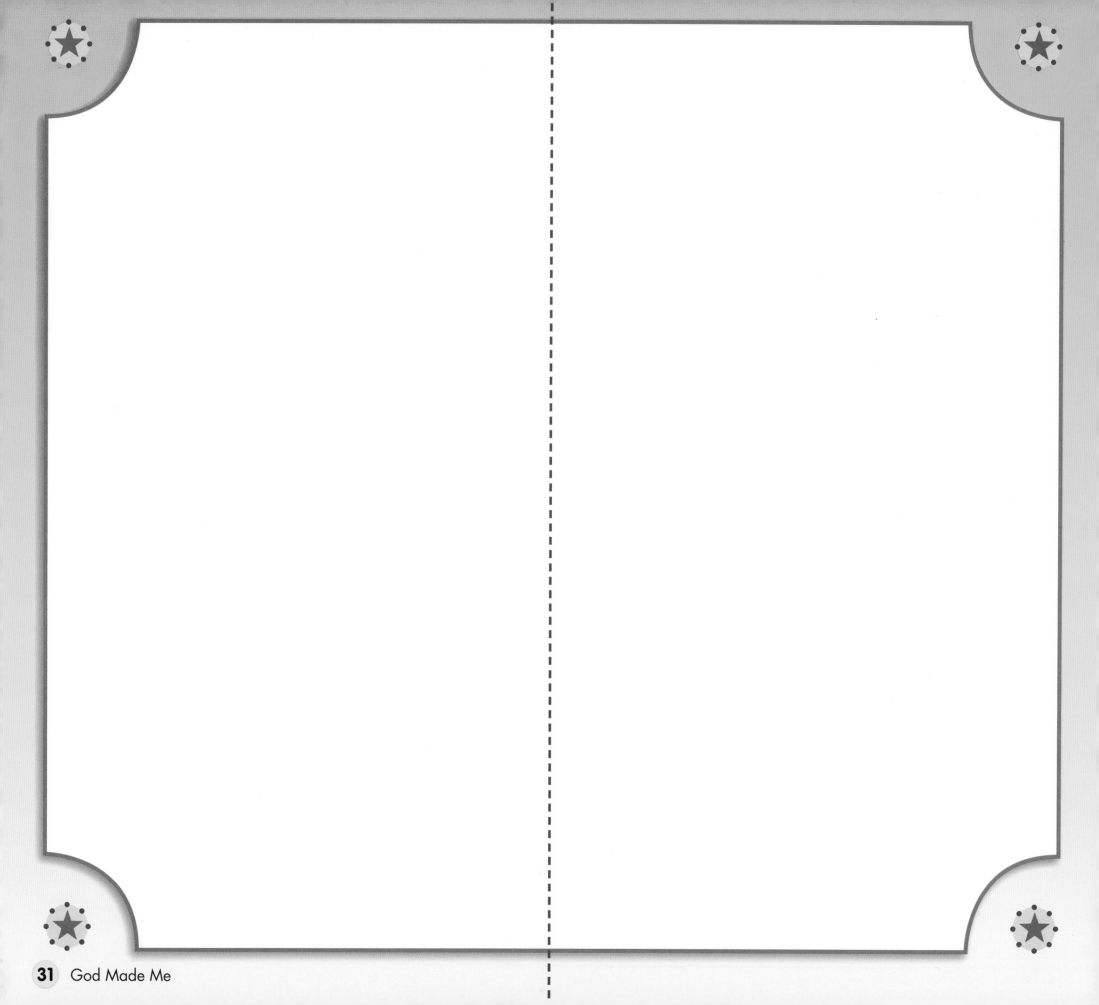

Name_____

© LOYOLA PRESS.

Name _____

Circle the children who are smiling.

Family Time

Chapter 10: I Can Smile

In this lesson the children reflected on being happy. They learned that God wants them to be happy, and they were encouraged to try to make others happy. Ask your child what Jesus did to make others happy. Decide where your child could display the smiling face received in class.

Your Child

Children are sensitive to your moods. Try to maintain your child's natural happiness and peace by smiling and being cheerful, especially when you do not feel like it. Enjoy your child's lightheartedness by joining in with his or her silly talk, jokes, and games. Use humor to smooth over difficult events and to persuade your child to obey.

Reflect

Sing joyfully to God, all people. Live for God with gladness. Come before God with joyful song. (adapted from Psalm 100:1–2.)

Pray

God, may we praise you with joy forever.

Do

- In the mornings greet your child cheerfully.
- Make smiling face cookies with your child.
- Spend a day with your child. Do what makes him or her happy.
- Greet your neighbors and smile.
- With your child, plan a surprise for a family member that will make him or her happy.
- When you and your child have had a happy experience, thank God aloud.
- Before your child goes to bed, recall the day's happy events.
- Read to your child *Where's Your Smile, Crocodile?* by Claire Freedman. Name ways to spread happiness. Thank God for all the people who share happiness with others.

For more family resources, refer to the Family Activity Booklet and visit **www.loyolapress.com/preschool.**

© LOYOLAPRESS.

© LOYOLA PRESS.

Name _____

Learn this sign language.

I love you.

Chapter 11: I Can Talk

In this lesson the children considered the gift of being able to talk, and they thanked God for their voices. They practiced saying polite words, using a megaphone they made. Ask your child what these polite words are. Tell your child "I love you" in the sign language shown.

Your Child

Children learn to speak through practice. Sometimes they talk to themselves, often during imaginative play. Spend time talking with your child. Correct your child's grammar by using the words correctly yourself.

Reflect

God, I will speak words of praise to you. (adapted from Psalm 51:17)

Pray

Jesus, Word of God, may we always speak words that are kind and true.

Do

- Let your child talk on the phone to a relative or friend.
- Play with rhyming words with your child. Say words (or nonwords) that rhyme, make up a rhyme, or have your child complete a rhyme.
- Tell your child stories about when you were young and invite him or her to tell you stories.
- Model polite expressions for your child, such as "please," "thank you," and "excuse me."
- Play store or house with your child and engage in make-believe conversations.
- Read poems and storybooks to your child and teach him or her nursery rhymes.
- Read to your child *Is Your Mama a Llama?* by Deborah Guarino. Describe a time when your child spoke politely to someone. Ask God to help you speak kindly to others.

For more family resources, refer to the Family Activity Booklet and visit **www.loyolapress.com/preschool.**

© LOYOLAPRESS.

Name

Touch each thing God made and say "I praise you."

Chapter 12: I Can Pray

In this lesson the children learned that they can talk to God through prayer. They recalled that God is everywhere and can hear us when we give praise or thanks. During the lesson the children prayed by themselves in their hearts and together as a group. The children were encouraged to pray in the morning and at night and made a doorknob hanger to remind them to pray. Help your child put the hanger on the doorknob of his or her room. Ask your child to explain the prayer book he or she made.

Your Child

Pray with your child spontaneously during the day to thank or praise God for something. In the morning and evening remind your child to thank God for the day. Let your child see you at prayer.

Reflect

Pray silently in your heart in secret. Your Father will hear you. (adapted from Matthew 6:6)

Pray

Jesus, teach us to pray with confidence and joy.

Do

- Have religious objects in your home as reminders of God.
- Begin the custom of a family prayer time.
- Thank God for your child.
- When your child is afraid or worried, remind him or her that God is there.
- Read a child's book of prayers or Bible stories to your child.
- Read to your child *Teach Me to Pray* by Pennie Kidd. Take turns giving examples of ways to pray anytime and anywhere. Ask your child to choose how he or she would like to pray with you right now.

For more family resources, refer to the Family Activity Booklet and visit **www.loyolapress.com/preschool.**

© LOYOLAPRESS.

God Made Me

Name _____

Find and circle the five singing birds.

Family Time

Chapter 13: I Can Sing

In this lesson the children talked about singing and learned that singing can be a form of prayer. They heard about the angel's visit to Mary and Mary's visit to Elizabeth when Mary sang to praise God. (Luke 1:46–56) They also heard that the angels sang "Glory to God in the highest" the night Jesus was born. (Luke 2:8–14) Ask your child to show you the angel he or she made.

Your Child

Encourage your child to sing and to enjoy music. Sing songs you make up yourself. Invite your child to make up songs. When you take your child to church, explain how music is part of the celebration. Point out the choir and any instruments used at Mass.

Reflect

I sing praise to the Lord; I rejoice in God my savior. (adapted from Luke 1:46)

Pray

God our Savior, we rejoice and sing praise to you!

Do

• Teach your child to sing a few children's songs.
• Ask your child to teach you a song learned in class.
• Wake up your child with a song and sing a lullaby at night.
• Make simple instruments for your child: Put tissue paper around a comb and hum or sing through it, with your mouth slightly open. Use a cylindrical container as a drum. Pour uncooked rice or beans into an empty shampoo bottle to make a shaker.
• Read to your child *All God's Critters Got a Place in the Choir* by Bill Staines. Ask your child to name or sing a favorite song. Choose a song or hymn to sing together as a prayer to God.

For more family resources, refer to the Family Activity Booklet and visit **www.loyolapress.com/preschool.**

© LOYOLAPRESS.

Name _____

© LOYOLAPRESS.

Draw lines from the child to the funny animals.

Chapter 14: I Can Laugh

In this lesson the children talked about laughing and about how God likes us to be happy and laugh. They learned that we laugh when something is funny. The children heard the story of Abraham and Sarah's boy named Isaac, whose name means "he laughs." (Genesis 17:15–19; 18:1–15; 21:1–7) Comment on the laughing face your child made.

Your Child

Enjoy your child's sense of humor. Cultivate it by laughing together frequently. Don't be disturbed when your child laughs at accidents such as those during which people fall or break things. This is typical behavior for three-year-olds, and in a short time it will change.

Reflect

Sarah then said, "God has given me cause to laugh, and all who hear of it will laugh with me." (Genesis 21:6)

Pray

God, open our hearts to receive your gift of joy.

Do

- Make your child laugh by making funny faces or by doing silly tricks.
- Point out to your child humorous scenes in daily life.
- Do something with your child that he or she likes to do.
- Make up silly stories with your child.
- Play a game where you and your child try to keep a straight face while staring at each other.
- Read to your child *Rosie's Walk* by Pat Hutchins. Take turns describing funny things that happened today. Thank God for the gift of laughter.

For more family resources, refer to the Family Activity Booklet and visit **www.loyolapress.com/preschool.**

© LOYOLAPRESS.

Name _____

© LOYOLAPRESS.

Draw green lines to match the shapes.

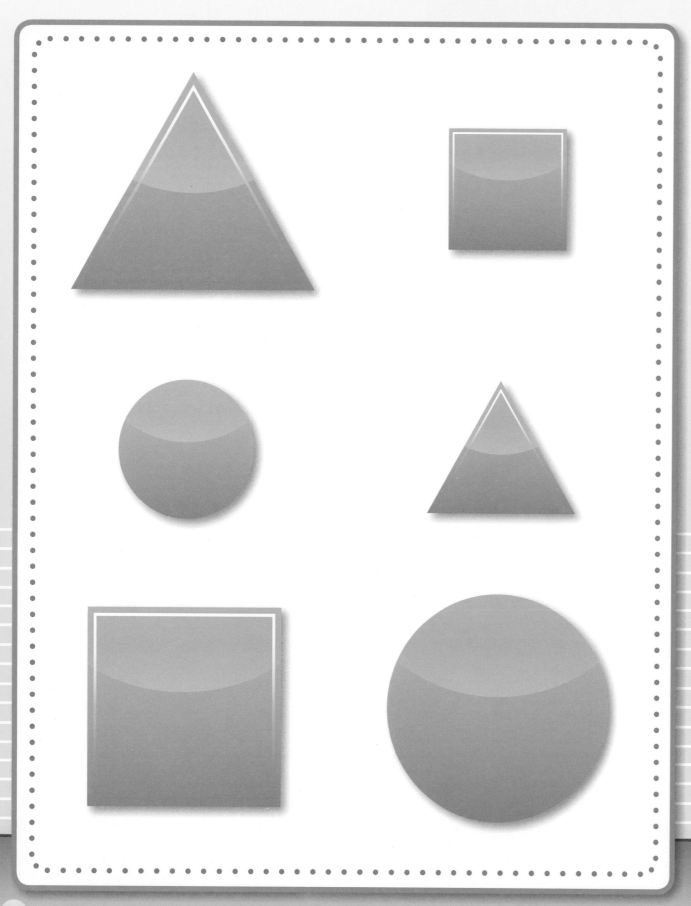

Chapter 15:
I Can Celebrate

In this lesson the children held a celebration and heard about Jesus' picnic for a crowd. (Mark 6:34–44) They celebrated the color green with green decorations, snacks, and flowers. On special occasions let your child wear the hat he or she made.

Your Child

Celebrating is characteristic of human beings. Celebrate birthdays and invite relatives and friends. Celebrate "ordinary" events: a child's losing the first tooth, a parent's new job, the arrival of a pet, or the first day of school. Include a prayer in the celebrations.

Reflect

The LORD is my shepherd;
  there is nothing I lack.
In green pastures you let me graze;
  to safe waters you lead me;
  you restore my strength. (Psalm 23:1–3)

Pray

Gracious God, we celebrate the wonder of your great love.

Do

- Celebrate anniversaries of sacraments. Establish rituals for the celebrations. Use special plates, sing a family song, or wear certain clothes.
- Celebrate holidays with a special meal or by getting together with relatives and friends.
- Celebrate whenever your child learns something new.
- Invite your child to suggest a reason for celebrating, especially on a gloomy day.
- Read to your child *If You Give a Pig a Party* by Laura Numeroff. Help your child to remember several recent family celebrations. Thank God for giving so many good reasons to celebrate.

For more family resources, refer to the Family Activity Booklet and visit **www.loyolapress.com/preschool.**

© LOYOLAPRESS.

Green Things I See

one bunch of grapes—
green, juicy, and mine!

Three green frogs
in green grass I see,

three green birds in
a big green tree,

three green turtles near
a dark green vine,

© LOYOLA PRESS.

Name

Add wheels to the pictures.

Family Time

Chapter 16: I Can Move

In this lesson the children, who at this age are energetic and active, thanked God for letting them move. They explored various ways they can move and reflected on the means of transportation that help them move from place to place. The children learned that they can use their movements to praise God, especially in dance. Play music and ask your child to demonstrate how to use the circle he or she made.

Your Child

Don't be surprised if your child regresses physically for a time. It is common for three-and-a-half-year-old children suddenly to become uncoordinated, to stutter, and to tremble. Provide plenty of opportunity for your child to exercise, play outside, and experiment with new types of activity.

Reflect

Miriam, the prophetess, led the women. Dancing and playing tambourines, they sang, "Sing to the Lord who is triumphant." (adapted from Exodus 15:20–21)

Pray

God, may we praise you in everything we do.

Do

- Take your child to a park or playground where he or she can run and play on the equipment.
- Drape a sheet over a few chairs to make a tent for your child. Play in it with him or her.
- Dance to music with your child.
- Challenge your child to new physical feats, such as hopping on one foot or skipping. Praise his or her efforts.
- Read to your child *Barn Dance!* by Bill Martin Jr. and John Archambault. Ask your child to name favorite playground activities. Thank God for the gift of movement.

For more family resources, refer to the Family Activity Booklet and visit **www.loyolapress.com/preschool.**

© LOYOLAPRESS.

Name _____

Find and circle the five hidden toys.

Chapter 17: I Can Play

In this lesson the children talked about playing and learned that God likes them to play. They were reminded to share and be kind as they play. They played the game "Squirrel in a Tree" and then made squirrel puppets and played with them. Play with the squirrel puppet at home. Have your child do the finger play he or she learned.

Your Child

Play is work for children. Through it they learn about the world and develop coordination and skills. Most three-year-olds are still in the stage of parallel play; that is, they play next to—but not with—one another. Gradually they begin to play together. Plan opportunities for your child to play with children close to his or her age, especially if your child has no siblings.

Reflect

I will praise the LORD with all my heart[.] (Psalm 111:1)

Pray

Father, renew our spirits that we may serve you with joy.

Do

- Play together as a family, especially on Sunday.
- Plan time to play individually with each child in your family.
- Provide homemade toys for your child: blocks from shoeboxes, a telescope out of a paper towel roll, a gigantic cardboard box to build a house.
- Consult books or other parents to find out about good children's games.
- Play a game that your child likes to play.
- Read to your child *William's Doll* by Charlotte Zolotow. Allow your child to talk about some favorite toys or games. Ask for God's help to share and play fairly with others.

For more family resources, refer to the Family Activity Booklet and visit **www.loyolapress.com/preschool.**

© LOYOLAPRESS.

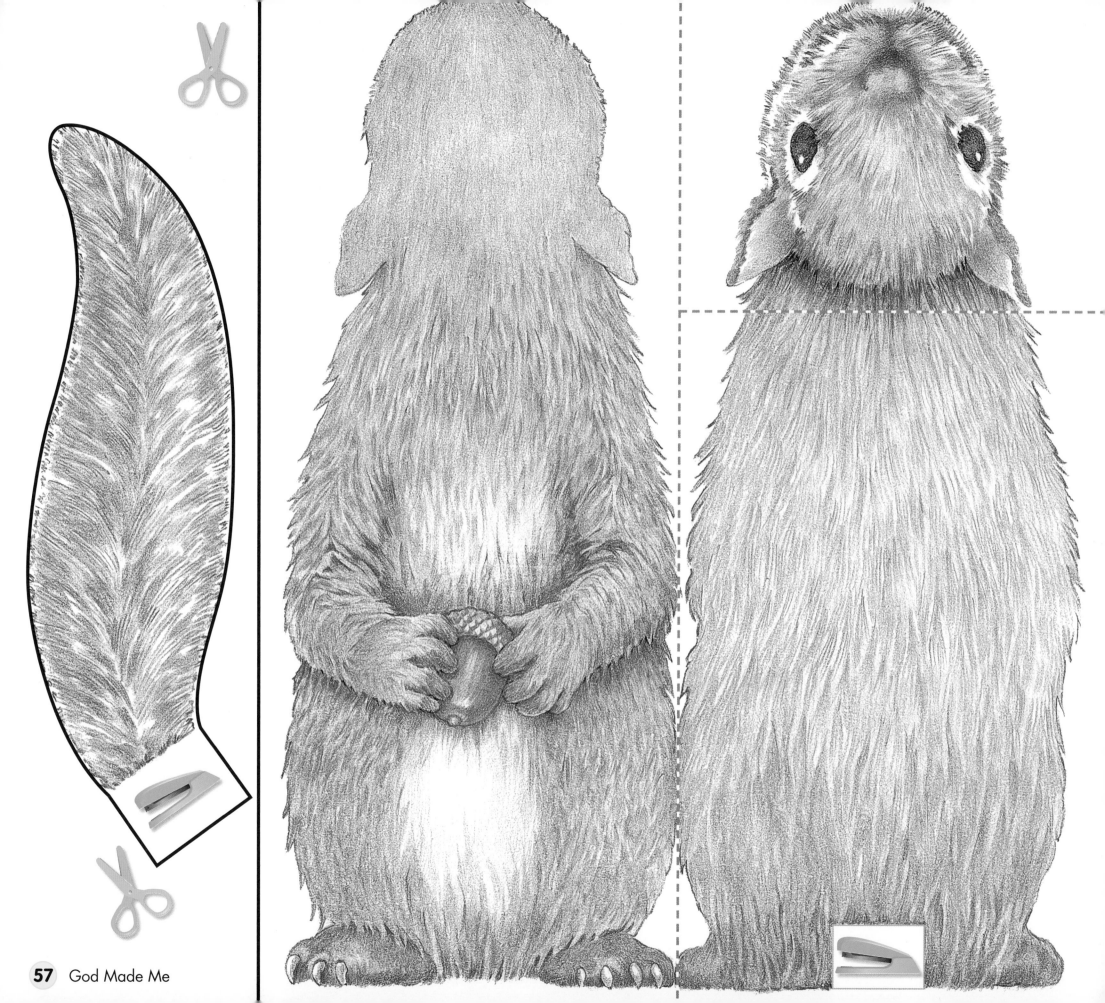

© LOYOLAPRESS.

Color Jesus and Joseph in the workshop.

Chapter 18: I Can Work

In this lesson the children considered how people work. They recalled how they themselves work and learned that Jesus worked as a teacher and as a carpenter. They worked hard to finish coloring a picture and to make a lovely piece of art. Commend your child for good work. Display the art where it can be seen and admired. Ask your child to tell you the story of the bees on the story card he or she received.

Your Child

Although your child finds satisfaction in work—which is in itself a reward—you might also praise and sometimes reward him or her for a job well done, or at least for the effort made.

Reflect

May God bless us and bless the work that we do. (adapted from Psalm 90:17)

Pray

God, may our love for you show forth in the work we do.

Do

- Explain to your child what you do at work or the work required around the house.
- Enlist your child's help in doing work around the house.
- With your child, watch construction workers, police officers, farmers, crossing guards, and other people at work.
- Sing with your child while you work around the house or yard.
- Reward yourself and your child with a special treat after a task is finished.
- Read to your child *The Very Busy Spider* by Eric Carle. Acknowledge your child's contributions to work around the house. Together ask God to bless all the work that you do.

For more family resources, refer to the Family Activity Booklet and visit **www.loyolapress.com/preschool.**

© LOYOLAPRESS.

Busy Bee made lots of honey.
Lazy Bee made none.
Now while Busy Bee is free,
Lazy's just begun.

4

Busy Bee and Lazy Bee

Busy Bee and Lazy Bee
Had work to be done.

1

Busy Bee got busy,
But Lazy Bee had fun.

Busy buzzed to many flowers
And worked on every one.
Lazy snoozed for hours and hours
In the nice, warm sun.

2

3

© LOYOLAPRESS.

Name_____

© LOYOLAPRESS.

Name _____

Finish the tree.

Chapter 19:
I Can Make Things

In this lesson the children learned that God made everything and has given us the ability to make things. They thanked God for various things in creation and considered how human beings can improve and beautify the world by taking care of it and by making things. During the lesson they made a necklace, a tree, and a dog.

Your Child

Children learn through manipulating objects. As they make things with play dough, crayons, and glue, they not only develop coordination and motor skills, but they also express their thoughts and feelings and show their talents. Three-year-olds are proud of their accomplishments. Give your child the satisfaction of making something new. Supply him or her with materials and ideas for creative projects.

Reflect

God saw everything he had made and called it very good. (adapted from Genesis 1:31)

Pray

God our Creator, make us good stewards of your creation.

Do

- Tour a city with your child to see what people have made.
- Make sculptures out of aluminum foil or paper.
- Let your child help make a meal.
- Help your child make homemade gifts.
- Have your child glue together stones or pieces of wood for a centerpiece or paint a clean, dry rock for a paperweight.
- Read to your child *Maisy Makes Lemonade* by Lucy Cousins. Show your child how he or she can create useful or beautiful things too. Thank God for the gift of creativity.

For more family resources, refer to the Family Activity Booklet and visit **www.loyolapress.com/preschool.**

© LOYOLAPRESS.

Draw lines to match the pictures.

Chapter 20: I Can Grow

In this lesson the children talked about growth. They learned that Jesus grew, just as they are growing. They considered how they have changed since they were babies and reviewed what makes them grow big and strong. Read to your child the page about growing. Place the chart he or she made where you will remember to record your child's height and weight each month. You might stand your child against a wall and draw a line to mark his or her height.

Your Child

Children enjoy growing and are proud of it. Make your child aware of his or her growth. Comment on new things your child can do because he or she has grown bigger and stronger. Avoid comparing your child to others or pointing out ways he or she is different from others. Three-year-olds do not like to be different.

Reflect

Jesus grew in age and wisdom.
(adapted from Luke 2:52)

Pray

Jesus, may we always grow stronger in our love for you.

Do

- Show your child pictures of you when you were a child.
- Show your child baby pictures and clothes he or she has outgrown. Tell stories about your child's baby days.
- Plant seeds and have your child watch them grow.
- Read to your child *Titch* by Pat Hutchins. Discuss ways your child is growing. Thank God for this continuing growth and maturity.

For more family resources, refer to the Family Activity Booklet and visit **www.loyolapress.com/preschool.**

© LOYOLAPRESS.

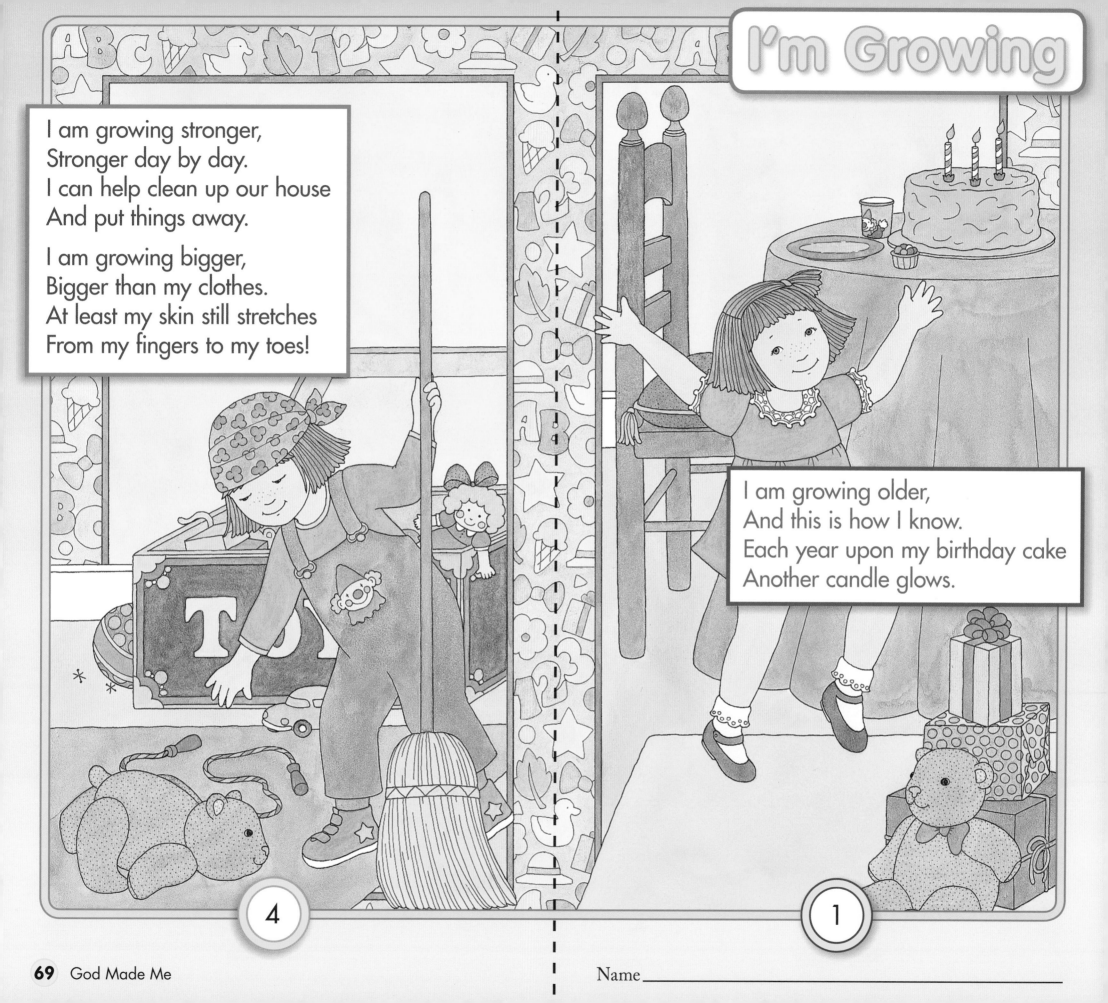

I am growing stronger,
Stronger day by day.
I can help clean up our house
And put things away.

I am growing bigger,
Bigger than my clothes.
At least my skin still stretches
From my fingers to my toes!

I am growing older,
And this is how I know.
Each year upon my birthday cake
Another candle glows.

4

1

Name _____

I am growing taller,
Not as tall as trees.
But now I come up higher
Than my father's knees.

I am growing wider,
For I no longer fit
In the baby's highchair
Where I used to sit.

I'm also growing heavy.
That's what my mother said
Last evening when she picked me up
To carry me to bed.

I am growing smarter.
I can count to three,
And sometimes I can even
Say my ABCs.

2

3

© LOYOLAPRESS.

_____

Date	Height	Weight

© LOYOLAPRESS.

Name_____

Draw a smiling face in the circle next to each happy child.

Chapter 21: I Can Feel

In this lesson the children learned about various feelings everyone has, including Jesus. They expressed these feelings by making faces and by dancing. The children were led to be sensitive to others' feelings. Have your child hang the lamb made in class on a doorknob and turn it to match his or her feelings.

Your Child

Three-year-olds are usually cheerful. They delight in the world, themselves, and new things. They are becoming aware of feelings. Help your child identify them by making comments such as "I see you are upset" or "You look worried." Remind your child that when he or she has unpleasant feelings, God cares. God loves him or her on good days and bad days.

Reflect

I have told you this so that my joy might be in you and your joy may be complete. This is my commandment: love one another as I love you. (John 15:11–12)

Pray

Jesus, may we know the joy that only you can give.

Do

- Assure your child that it is all right to cry when we are sad or hurt.
- Comment on the feelings of characters in books and shows.
- Point out how your child's actions may make others feel.
- Accept an apology from your child with a hug, saying "I forgive you and I love you." Apologize yourself.
- Read to your child *When I Feel Angry* by Cornelia Maude Spelman. Talk with your child about appropriate ways to express feelings. Thank God for loving us always.

For more family resources, refer to the Family Activity Booklet and visit **www.loyolapress.com/preschool.**

© LOYOLAPRESS.

Name _____

© LOYOLAPRESS.

Name _____

Draw a circle around the people you want to pray for.

Chapter 22: I Can Wish

In this lesson the children learned about wishes. They recalled times when people make wishes, and they shared some of their own wishes. They learned that God wishes only what is best for them and that we can send best wishes to others. Ask your child to show you the story about Benny Bunny who worked to make his wish come true. Your child made a card expressing best wishes for someone. Help deliver it if necessary.

Your Child

Pay close attention when your child expresses a wish. Help him or her distinguish between wishes that can really come true and those that are impossible. Your child's wishes may reveal his or her fears.

Reflect

"If you then . . . know how to give good gifts to your children, how much more will your heavenly Father give good things to those who ask him." (Matthew 7:11)

Pray

Heavenly Father, we thank you for your goodness and love.

Do

- Share with your child what you wish for him or her.
- Bless your child with the Sign of the Cross on his or her forehead each night.
- At a family gathering have each person complete the statement "I wish . . ."
- Tell your child a story about someone who made wishes.
- Read to your child *The Little Engine That Could* by Watty Piper. Talk about a time your child completed a difficult task. Give thanks to God who always helps us and wants the best for us.

For more family resources, refer to the Family Activity Booklet and visit www.loyolapress.com/preschool.

© LOYOLA PRESS.

Finally Benny Bunny had a beautiful garden in his yard. His wish had come true.

4

Benny Bunny's Wish

Benny Bunny lived next door to Betty Bunny. She had many pretty flowers in her front yard.

"Mom," said Benny Bunny one morning, "I wish we had pretty flowers like those in Betty Bunny's yard."

"No problem," said Mommy Bunny. "We will have to do some planting."

1

Name_____

Mommy Bunny and Benny Bunny went to the store. They bought some flower seeds.

That afternoon Mommy Bunny and Benny Bunny cleared a patch of ground. They pulled weeds and made the soil soft. Then they planted the flower seeds and watered them well.

Every day the sun shined, and Benny Bunny watered the seeds. Soon green shoots began to peek through the dirt. The shoots grew tall and put out leaves and then buds and then flowers!

2

3

© LOYOLAPRESS.

© LOYOLA PRESS.

_____

Name_____

Color the letter O.

Chapter 23: I Can Learn

In this lesson the children heard that they are more special than animals because God gave them the ability to think. They reviewed many of the things they have learned since they were babies. The children were led to realize that they are learning more about God. Ask your child what he or she has learned about God. Admire the spiral design or place mat your child made.

Your Child

Three-year-old children delight in learning things. Help your child acquire new skills and knowledge. As you do so, you are building his or her self-esteem. Be patient in answering when your child asks "Why?" thereby adding to his or her understanding of the world. Teach your child to persevere when things are difficult.

Reflect

Take my yoke upon you and learn from me, for I am meek and humble of heart; and you will find rest for yourselves. (Matthew 11:29)

Pray

Jesus, may we learn to follow your way of love.

Do

- Mention it to your child when you notice that he or she has learned something new.
- Occasionally ask your child what he or she is thinking.
- Give your child choices in clothes, foods, games, or books to be read.
- Teach your child something new this week.
- Ask your child to recite a poem or sing a song he or she knows.
- Read to your child *Froggy Learns to Swim* by Jonathan London. Help your child name some of the many things he or she is learning. Thank God for the ability to think and learn.

For more family resources, refer to the Family Activity Booklet and visit **www.loyolapress.com/preschool.**

© Loyola Press.

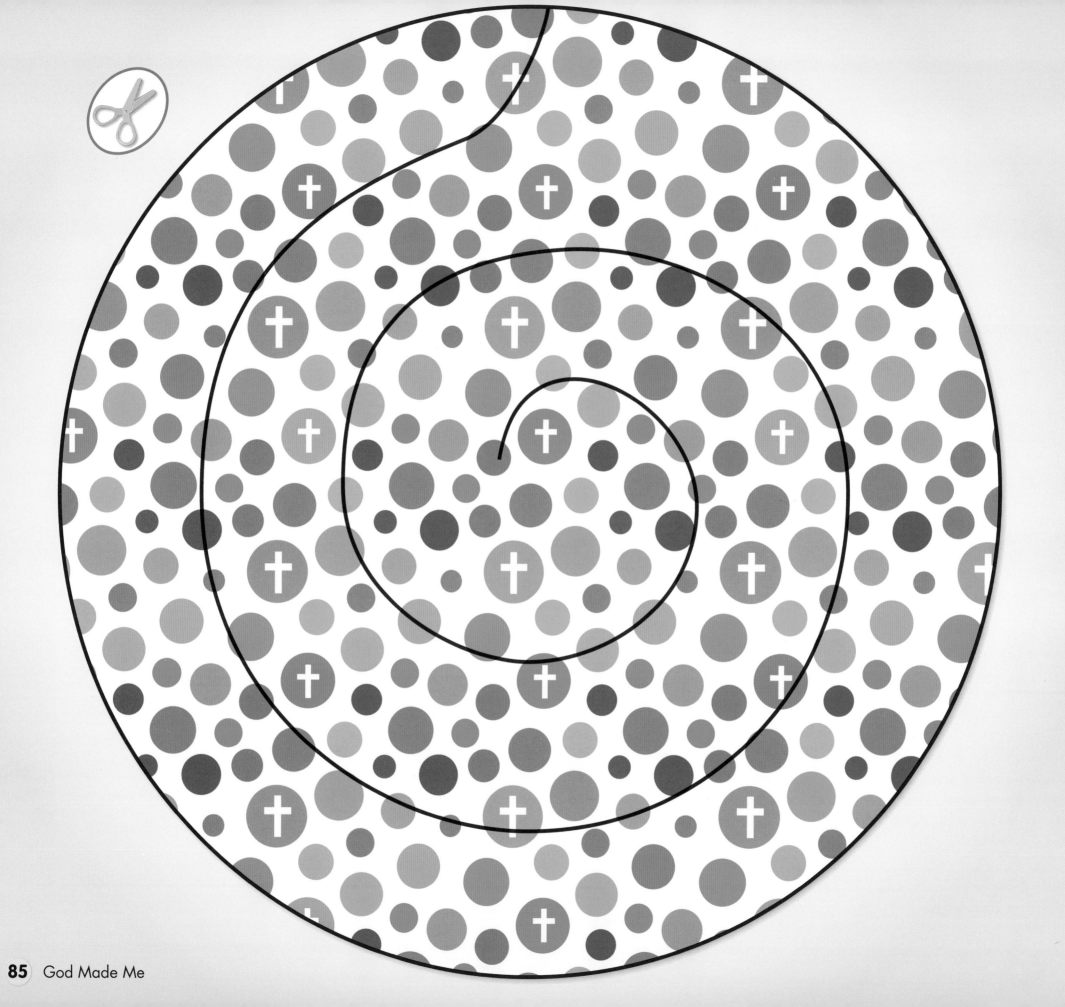

Name _____

© LOYOLA PRESS.

Name _____

Circle the make-believe things.

Chapter 24:
I Can Pretend

In this lesson the children experienced pretending. They played house, made believe they were performing certain actions, and pretended they were on a lion hunt. The children learned that God made them to enjoy pretending. Be creative in making up games to play with the lion your child made. You might pretend that the lion can talk or that he is a guest.

Your Child

Pretending is essential to children's play. It is one way children learn to cope with the world and practice skills. If your child has an imaginary friend, join in the fun instead of fighting it.

Reflect

I praise you that I am wonderfully made. (adapted from Psalm 139:14)

Pray

God our Creator, we praise you for the gifts of imagination and creativity.

Do

- Let your child dress up in grown-ups' clothes.
- Play games, such as store and house, with your child.
- While driving in the car, pretend it is something else, such as a rocket or a submarine.
- Give your child a huge cardboard box or several cartons to play with imaginatively.
- Read or tell your child some fairy tales.
- Play a game of charades with your child.
- Read to your child *Where the Wild Things Are* by Maurice Sendak. Have fun describing imaginary creatures to one another. Thank God for the gift of imagination.

For more family resources, refer to the Family Activity Booklet and visit **www.loyolapress.com/preschool.**

© LOYOLAPRESS.

Name _____

Color the hearts by the children who are showing love.

Chapter 25: I Can Love

In this lesson the children talked about the greatest thing that God enables us to do: love. They made a gift for someone they love and talked about God and others who love them. They thought of ways to show their love for people. Help your child deliver his or her gift if necessary. Your child made a love pocket containing three hearts that represent three ways to show love—hugs and kisses, the words "I love you," and loving deeds. Each night you can help your child use these hearts to decide whether he or she has shown love that day.

Your Child

God's love is communicated to your child through the love of your family. Assure your child often of your love. Point out ways that he or she can show love.

Reflect

Love one another as I love you.
(adapted from John 13:34)

Pray

Jesus, help us to love others as you love us.

Do

- Plan with your child a way to show love for a grandparent.
- Tell your child why you love him or her.
- Point out to your child signs of God's love for him or her.
- Take your child on an errand for a neighbor, or when you take a gift to someone who is ill or needs cheering up.
- Read to your child *I Love You More* by Laura Duksta. Talk about ways your family shows love in words and actions. Thank God for helping us show love to others.

For more family resources, refer to the Family Activity Booklet and visit **www.loyolapress.com/preschool.**

© LOYOLAPRESS.

Name

© LOYOLAPRESS.

Color Jesus' friend, Saint Paul.

Family Time

Special Lesson 1:
Halloween/Feast of All Saints

In this lesson the children learned that Halloween ("hallows' eve") is the beginning of a religious celebration. It is the eve of the Feast of All Saints, the friends of Jesus. The children learned about Saint Paul, a great saint who wrote letters about Jesus and preached the Gospel on his many travels. Then they participated in a parade as friends of Jesus. On Halloween night display the lantern your child made.

Your Child
Assure your child that ghosts, goblins, and witches are all in fun. Enjoy dressing up your child for Halloween. Dress up yourself.

Reflect
Be kind to one another.
(adapted from Ephesians 4:32)

Pray
Jesus, help us to live as your friend.

Do
• Tell your child about his or her patron saint or another saint, such as the saint of your parish.
• Hold a simple Halloween party at your home. Involve your child in the preparations.
• Let your child decide what he or she wants to be for Halloween.
• Have your child at the door to see and enjoy the visitors who come for treats.
• Carve a pumpkin for your child or bake a pumpkin pie.
• Read to your child *The Biggest Pumpkin Ever* by Steven Kroll. Talk about things that help us grow to be friends of Jesus. Pray for God's help to live always as Jesus' friends.

For more family resources, refer to the Family Activity Booklet and visit **www.loyolapress.com/preschool.**

© LOYOLAPRESS.

Name _____

Find and circle the seven hidden gifts.

Family Time

Special Lesson 2: Advent

In this lesson the children were introduced to Advent as a time of waiting for Christmas, the celebration of God's love and Jesus' birthday. They were encouraged to give Jesus their love. During Advent, display the wreath your child made.

Your Child

Center your celebration of Christmas on its true meaning. Try to avoid the consumerism that marks its secular celebration. Obtain a nativity set if you do not already have one. Have family members try to do one loving thing each day to prepare for Christmas, the feast of love.

Reflect

The angel said to Mary, "You will have a son and you shall name him Jesus. He will be great and will be called the Son of God."
(adapted from Luke 1:30–32)

Pray

God, prepare our hearts to welcome your Son, Jesus.

Do

• Pray a special Advent prayer before dinner, such as "O come, O come, Emmanuel."
• Help your child make gifts for family members and friends.
• Involve your child in Christmas preparations, such as baking cookies, sending Christmas cards, and decorating the house.
• Teach your child two or three Christmas carols.
• Display an empty manger from your nativity set as a reminder that Jesus is coming.
• Mark off each day until Christmas on a calendar.
• Read to your child *Waiting for Christmas: A Story about the Advent Calendar* by Kathleen Long Bostrom. Discuss how your family prepares for Christmas. Ask God to help your family prepare to celebrate Christmas with joy.

For more family resources, refer to the Family Activity Booklet and visit **www.loyolapress.com/preschool.**

© LOYOLAPRESS.

Put lights and ornaments on the tree.

Family Time

Special Lesson 3:
Christmas

In this lesson the children heard the story of the first Christmas. They talked about celebrating Christmas at home and then had a short prayer service around a nativity set. Ask your child to tell you the story of Jesus' birth, looking at the picture on page 97.

Your Child

On Christmas Day try to keep your child focused on Jesus, God's gift to us, more than on other gifts he or she receives. Stress that Christmas is a feast of love. Establish family Christmas customs now that will make treasured memories for your child later. Traditions give children a sense of security and teach them values.

Reflect

Mary gave birth to her firstborn son, wrapped him in swaddling clothes, and laid him in a manger. (adapted from Luke 2:7)

Pray

God, help us to celebrate Christmas as a feast of love.

Do

- With your child go through the Christmas cards you received. Pray for those who sent them.
- Play religious Christmas songs for your child.
- Read aloud the story of the first Christmas from Luke 2:1–20. Your child will come to understand it gradually.
- Read to your child *Saint Francis Celebrates Christmas* by Mary Caswell Walsh. Have your child tell you the part of the story of Jesus' birth he or she likes best. Pray together by singing a Christmas hymn.

For more family resources, refer to the Family Activity Booklet and visit **www.loyolapress.com/preschool.**

© LOYOLAPRESS.

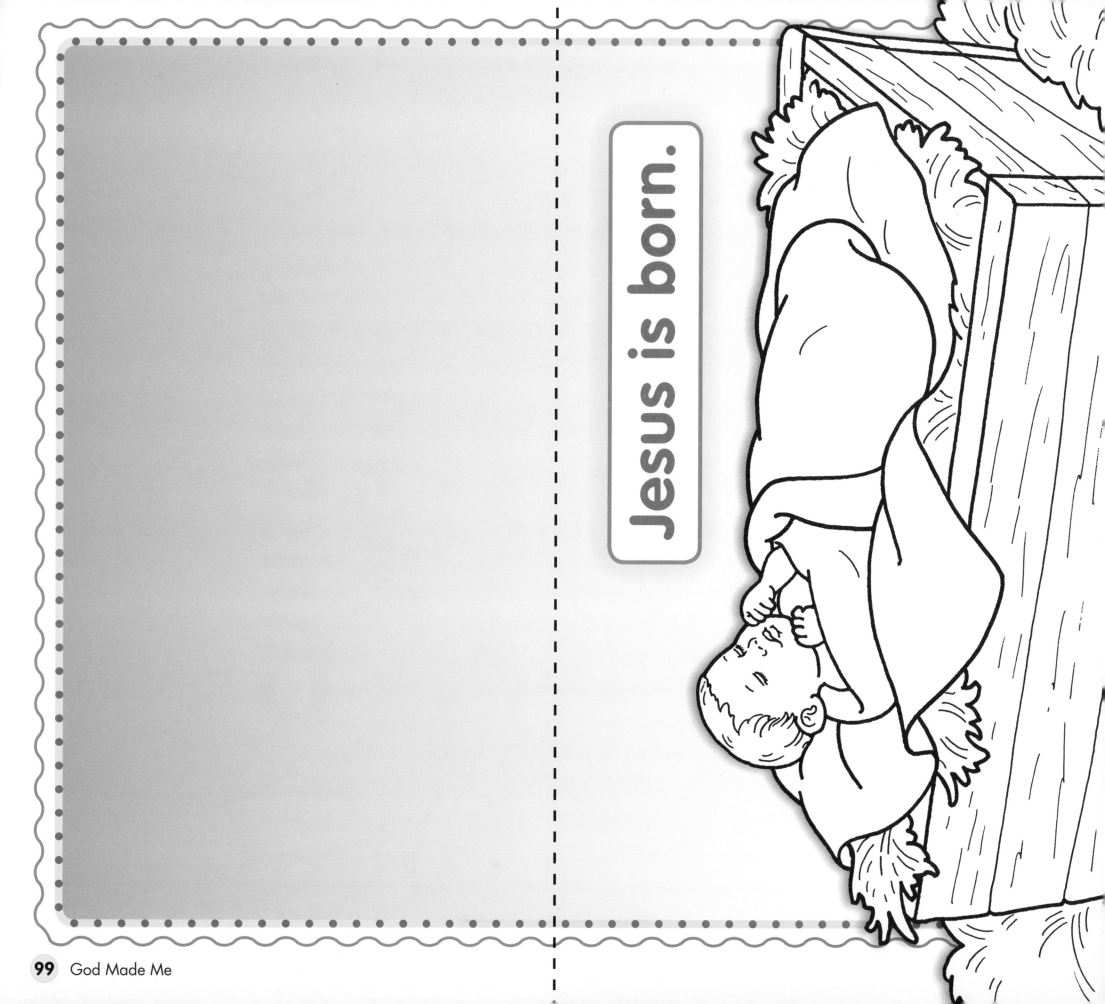

Jesus is born.

© LOYOLAPRESS.

1

2

3

Circle the things that will help flowers to grow.

Special Lesson 4: Lent

In this lesson the children were introduced to Lent, a time to grow in God's love as we prepare to celebrate Easter. They talked about how seeds grow into plants. They heard Jesus' words about seeds dying to produce much fruit. Ask your child about the seeds he or she planted. If this was brought home, help your child care for the seedlings as they grow.

Your Child

Lent often corresponds to the change of seasons from winter to spring. Observing signs of new life in the natural world around them prepares children to later comprehend the significance of Jesus' Passion, Death, and Resurrection. Especially during Lent, take time to help your child notice nature's transformation from death to new life.

Reflect

Unless a seed falls to the ground and dies, it remains just a seed; but if it dies, it produces much fruit. (adapted from John 12:24)

Pray

Jesus, help us to grow always in God's love.

Do

- Allow your child to help with springtime gardening activities.
- Tie two twigs to make a cross. Set it in dirt in a flowerpot or cup. Help your child plant grass seeds around the cross.
- Display a cross or crucifix during Lent and include a special Lenten prayer at mealtimes or at bedtime.
- Read to your child *The Carrot Seed* by Ruth Krauss. Talk with your child about seeds and other signs of new life you see in spring. Pray together thanking God for these signs of new life.

For more family resources, refer to the Family Activity Booklet and visit **www.loyolapress.com/preschool.**

© LOYOLAPRESS.

Name_____

> Draw flowers in the grass and blossoms in the tree.

Family Time

Special Lesson 5: Easter

In this lesson the children learned that Easter is a celebration of new life. They talked about new life seen in the spring, such as baby animals, flowers, and butterflies. They told and sang about what they can do because they are alive. Although three-year-olds are too young to comprehend that Jesus died and rose again, they are led to associate him with new life. Hang the butterfly your child made in a conspicuous place.

Your Child

As young children experience surprise and joy at finding an Easter basket early Sunday morning, they share the emotions of the first Christians who witnessed Christ's Easter miracle. Enjoy the beauty and freshness of the Easter season with your child. Take a walk or play in a park.

Reflect

I came to give you life. (adapted from John 10:10)

Pray

Jesus, fill us with joy and hope.

Do

- Arrange to have your child observe new life, such as chicks, bunnies, or spring flowers.
- Have your child assist you in decorating Easter eggs.
- Let your child help select a new outfit to wear on Easter.
- Teach your child the bunny hop.
- Put a picture or symbol of Jesus in your child's Easter basket.
- Read to your child *Easter* by Gail Gibbons. Talk about the ways your family celebrates Easter. Praise God for the joy of Easter.

For more family resources, refer to the Family Activity Booklet and visit **www.loyolapress.com/preschool.**

© LOYOLAPRESS.

Name _____

Match the pictures to show how air moves things.

Family Time

Special Lesson 6:
Pentecost

We celebrate the gift of the Holy Spirit on Pentecost. This lesson prepared the children to appreciate the work of the Holy Spirit in our lives. They learned about air and its presence all around us. They learned that God's presence with us is like the air: God is everywhere and with us always.

Your Child

As young children grow in their understanding of God, they take comfort in knowing that God is everywhere. Remind your child often that God is always with him or her.

Reflect

The spirit of the Lord fills the whole world. (adapted from Wisdom 1:7)

Pray

Holy Spirit, fill us with your life and love.

Do

- On a breezy day, take a walk with your child and notice the wind's power.
- Enjoy flying a kite or blowing bubbles with your child.
- Hang a decorative flag, windsock, or wind chime outside to help your child observe the effects of the wind.
- Read to your child *The Wind Blew* by Pat Hutchins. Ask your child to name some things the wind can do. Together thank God for being with us always.

For more family resources, refer to the Family Activity Booklet and visit **www.loyolapress.com/preschool.**

© LOYOLA PRESS.

Name

© LOYOLAPRESS.

Name_____

Trace the path past things we thank God for.

Family Time

Special Lesson 7:
Thanksgiving

In this lesson the children were introduced to Thanksgiving as a day to thank God for everything. They heard that we celebrate all God's gifts by a special meal. They learned that a cornucopia filled with food is a Thanksgiving decoration. Use the cornucopia your child made to decorate your home for Thanksgiving. Plan with him or her to say a Thanksgiving prayer before your meal.

Your Child

Help form a thankful heart in your child by pointing out things for which to be thankful. Prompt him or her to give thanks to God and to others. Express thanks yourself, not forgetting to thank your child when it is appropriate.

Reflect

I thank you, LORD, with all my heart[.]
(Psalm 138:1)

Pray

God, we thank you for all your wonderful gifts.

Do

- Let your child help with Thanksgiving preparations.
- Have your child draw things he or she is thankful for or glue pictures of them on paper or on a paper plate.
- Take your child to a farm or to a grocery store to see the great variety in our foods.
- Go for a drive and, as you go, pray a litany of Thanksgiving for what you see on the way.
- Read to your child *Thanksgiving Is. . .* by Gail Gibbons. Talk about how your family celebrates Thanksgiving. Take turns naming things for which you are thankful and pray "We thank you, God" after each is named.

For more family resources, refer to the Family Activity Booklet and visit **www.loyolapress.com/preschool.**

© LOYOLAPRESS.

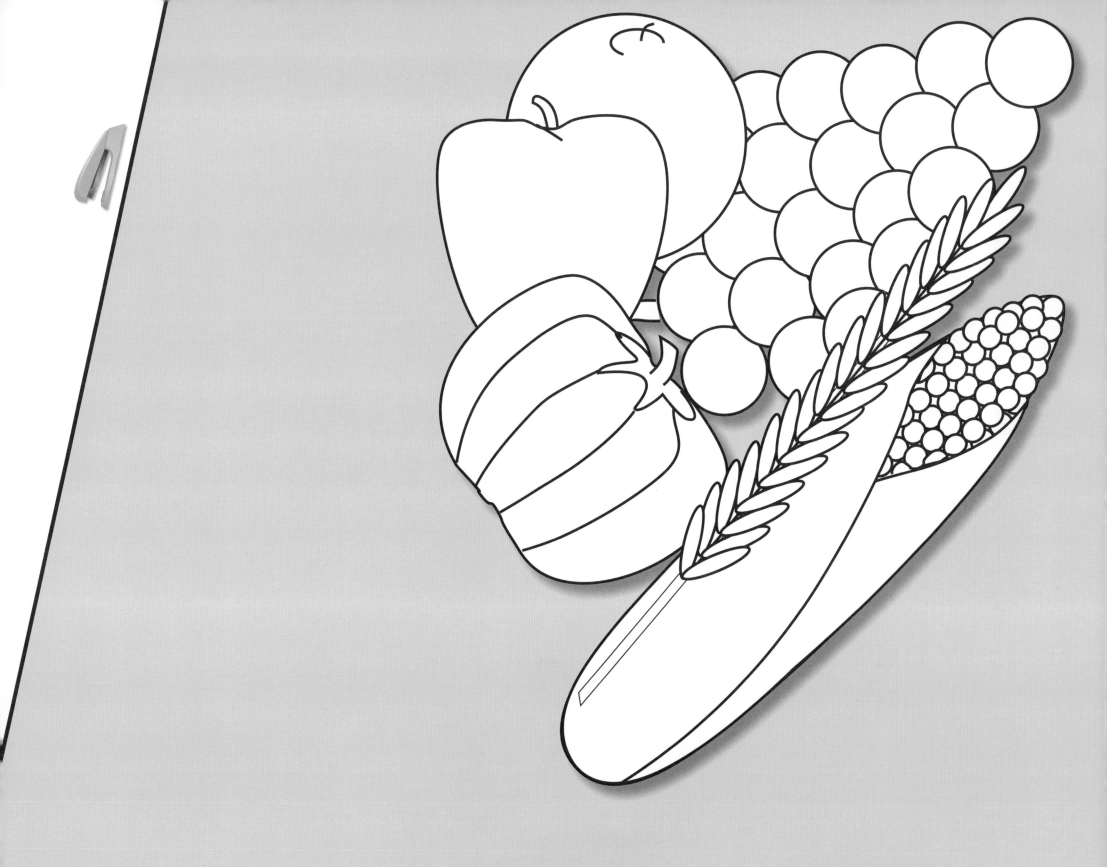

God Made Me

© LOYOLAPRESS.

Name_____

Draw lines to match the hearts that are the same.

Special Lesson 8:
Valentine's Day

In this lesson the children learned that Valentine's Day is a day to show love. They recalled God's great love for them. They talked about people who love them and how they can show love for others. Admire the giant valentine your child made. Help deliver it if necessary.

Your Child

Being loved is essential to a child's moral and emotional development. Through your words and actions make sure that your child perceives himself or herself as lovable. Make every day a Valentine's Day at home.

Reflect

See, I have written your name on the palms of my hands. (adapted from Isaiah 49:16)

Pray

God, we praise you for your great love.

Do

- Hold a Valentine's Day party in your home for your child and a few of your child's friends.
- Serve pink or red drinks and dessert on Valentine's Day.
- Give your child a valentine.
- Go with your child to take a valentine to someone who doesn't expect it.
- Make a Valentine's Day phone call with your child to someone special, such as a grandparent.
- Give the gift of yourself to your child on Valentine's Day by doing something together.
- Read to your child *Valentine Surprise* by Corinne Demas. Choose something special to do together to show love to your family for Valentine's Day. Pray in thanks to God who always loves us.

For more family resources, refer to the Family Activity Booklet and visit **www.loyolapress.com/preschool.**

© LOYOLAPRESS.

Because you mean so much to me,

I made this valentine for you.

It says I love you with all my heart.

I hope you love me too.

_____

Draw lines to match the babies with their mothers.

Family Time

Special Lesson 9:
Mother's Day

In this lesson the children talked about their mothers and learned that Mary, the mother of Jesus, is also their mother in heaven. They were encouraged to show love and appreciation for their mothers on earth and for their mother, Mary, in heaven. They thanked God for their mother and for giving them Mary as their mother.

Your Child

Three-year-olds are typically very dependent on their mothers. They love being with their mothers and doing things with them. However, at age three-and-a-half they may experience a period of rebellion. Your child needs your patience and understanding as he or she learns to deal with life and cope with the challenges of being human.

Reflect

Jesus went with Mary and Joseph to Nazareth and obeyed them. Mary remembered all these things in her heart. (adapted from Luke 2:51)

Pray

Generous God, bless all mothers and strengthen them with your love and grace.

Do

• Display in your home a picture or statue of Mary.
• Talk with your child about what Mary must have done for Jesus when he was your child's age.
• Tell your child stories about when you were little and what your mother did for you.
• Visit a zoo or farm at a time when you can see mother animals and their babies.
• Read to your child *On Mother's Lap* by Ann Herbert Scott. Ask your child to describe something a mother does to show love for her child. Ask God to bless all mothers and those who love and care for others.

For more family resources, refer to the Family Activity Booklet and visit **www.loyolapress.com/preschool.**

© LOYOLA PRESS.

or

Happy Mother's Day!

or

© LOYOLAPRESS.

Trace the path from the girl to her father.

Family Time

Special Lesson 10:
Father's Day

In this lesson the children learned that Father's Day is a day to show love for their fathers and to thank them for all they do. They talked about their fathers and acted out what they do with their fathers. They heard that Jesus called God "our Father in heaven."

Your Child

Tell your child from time to time how much God loves him or her. Whenever something good happens or you and your child see something wonderful, remind your child to thank and praise God, our loving Father, for it. This will help your child live a good moral life not because of the fear of punishment but because of the desire to maintain his or her love relationship with the good God.

Reflect

This is how you are to pray: Our Father in heaven, hallowed be your name. . .
(Matthew 6:9)

Pray

God our Father, bless all fathers and encourage them with your steadfast love.

Do

- Plan something special for your child's grandfathers or great-grandfathers.
- Talk about the role of Saint Joseph in the Holy Family.
- Help your child make a gift for his or her father.
- Address family prayers to God our Father.
- Read to your child *Emma's Pet* by David McPhail. Ask your child to describe something a father does to show love for his child. Ask God to bless all fathers and those who love and care for others.

For more family resources, refer to the Family Activity Booklet and visit **www.loyolapress.com/preschool.**

© LOYOLAPRESS.

This is to certify that
you are one of
the world's greatest dads.

Happy Father's Day!

_____

© LOYOLA PRESS.

Name _____

Trace the dotted lines to make balloons. Color the balloons.

Family Time

Special Lesson 11: Birthdays

In this lesson the children celebrated life, their own lives in particular. They held a birthday party for everyone that included gifts and small cakes. They recalled that they are God's children and that God loves them very much. Save the birthday cape that your child made. It can be worn on his or her real birthday.

Your Child

Instill in your child respect for life by showing reverence for all people and all living things.

Reflect

I have called you by name . . . (Isaiah 43:1)

Pray

God, we praise you for the gift of life.

Do

- Ask your child what he or she likes best about being alive.
- Point out the beauty of a baby's little features to your child.
- After an enjoyable activity with your child, comment on how wonderful it is to be alive.
- Make your child aware of the many different types of people in the world. Introduce him or her to some of them or invite some of them to your home.
- Come up with some family rituals for celebrating birthdays.
- Read to your child *Happy Birthday, Dear Duck* by Jan Brett. Share favorite memories of your child's birthdays and other celebrations. Pray in thanks for the day of your child's birth.

For more family resources, refer to the Family Activity Booklet and visit **www.loyolapress.com/preschool.**

© LOYOLAPRESS.

I am special!

_____

© LOYOLAPRESS.

Name _____

Draw something you will enjoy this summer.

Special Lesson 12:
Last Class/Summer

In this lesson the children talked about their summer activities. They were reminded that whatever they do, God is there with them, caring for them and loving them. They also recalled what they learned in preschool. Ask your child to show you the certificate he or she received. Congratulate your child and display the certificate.

Your Child

During the summer bring out some of the cards and crafts from this preschool program and review with your child what he or she has learned. Do several of the finger plays and songs from the Family Activity Booklet.

Reflect

The Lord is kind and full of love. (adapted from Psalm 145:8)

Pray

Gracious God, we thank you for your never-ending love and care.

Do

- Continue to pray spontaneously with your child over the summer as you enjoy good times together.
- Plan family activities, such as a family picnic, a family trip, and family games.
- Go to local festivals and fairs as a family.
- Keep a family scrapbook of the summer's activities.
- Have your family portrait taken.
- Read to your child *Summersaults* by Douglas Florian. Talk about some of the fun things your family will do this summer. Ask God to bless your family and your summertime activities.

For more family resources, refer to the Family Activity Booklet and visit **www.loyolapress.com/preschool.**

© LOYOLAPRESS.

This is to certify that

_____

has completed the _God Made Me_ preschool program.

_____   _____
Catechist's Signature   **Date**

© LOYOLAPRESS.

Family Time

LIVING AND EXPERIENCING FAITH AT HOME is key to your child's faith formation. After each chapter, your child will bring home "Family Time," a feature that provides essential tools to help you live your faith as a family.

For more faith development opportunities, visit

www.loyolapress.com/preschool

LOYOLAPRESS.
A JESUIT MINISTRY

(16)

This booklet will help you enrich lessons from your child's preschool religion class. The following poems, finger plays, and songs are for your family to enjoy at home. If a craft is to be completed at home, help your child follow the directions.

Chapter 1: I Can Hear

Song
To the tune of "Mary Had a Little Lamb":
I have ears so I can hear, I can hear, I can hear.   [Put hands behind ears.]
I have ears so I can hear.
God made me   [Put thumbs in shoulders.]
wonderful!   [Raise arms.]
Mary Kathleen Glavich, S.N.D.

Craft
Name Tag (page 1)
Cut out the heart and write your name on the line. Staple or tape yarn or ribbon to the heart so it can be worn.

Chapter 2: I Can See

Song
Same tune as above, using the words:
"I have eyes so I can see."

Craft
Magic Window (perforated Card A)
Decorate the front side of the perforated card with crayons or markers. Punch out the three sides of the rectangle on the card and fold the flap back to make a window to see through.

Chapter 3: I Can Smell

Song
Same tune as above, using the words:
"I've a nose so I can smell."

Craft
Flowers (page 9)
Paint flowers on the stems, using sponges dipped in tempera paint and held with clothespins. (Or print with objects such as lids, cookie cutters, spools, or old toothbrushes.) Glue cotton balls in the center of the flowers and add perfume to them.

Special Lesson 10: Father's Day

Craft
Scroll for Father's Day (page 123)
Write your name on the line. Decorate the scroll. If you wish, glue on a picture of yourself or draw a self-portrait. Roll the scroll and put a rubber band or a piece of ribbon or yarn around it. Give it to your father on Father's Day.

Special Lesson 11: Birthdays

Song
To the tune of "Happy Birthday":
Oh, we thank you we do.
Oh, we thank you we do.
Oh, we thank you, dear God.
Oh, we thank you, we do.

Craft
Birthday Cape (page 127)
Punch holes in the card and tie an 8-inch piece of ribbon to each hole. Write your name on the line. Decorate the cape with crayons or markers or by gluing on magazine pictures of things you enjoy in life. If you wish, staple crepe-paper streamers along the bottom of the cape.

Special Lesson 12: Last Class/Summer

Poem
God Is There
When I run in the sun,
God is there. God is there.
When I fall playing ball,
God cares. God cares.
When I'm sad or I'm glad,
God knows. God knows.
When I mind or I'm kind,
God sees. God sees.
God is with me day and night,
Helping me to do what's right.
I love you, God!
Mary Kathleen Glavich, S.N.D.

Special Lesson 7: Thanksgiving

Craft

Cornucopia (page 111)

Color or paint the fruits and vegetables. Bend the card to form a horn and staple the sides together.

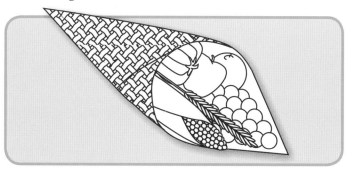

Special Lesson 8: Valentine's Day

Craft

Valentine (page 115)

Decorate the card as a giant valentine for someone you love by gluing on scraps of paper, foil, glitter, sequins, rickrack, ribbon, or lace. Sign the card, and if you wish, add Xs and Os to represent kisses and hugs.

Special Lesson 9: Mother's Day

Craft

Notepaper Holder/Mother's Day Card (page 119)

Cut apart the card and the notepaper holder. Decorate the yellow sides of the greeting card and the paper holder by making designs with kitchen objects dipped in tempera paint. When the paint is dry, fold the card and sign it. Fold the holder so that the decoration is on the front. Staple or glue the sides of the holder together. Punch a hole at the top of the paper holder and string yarn or ribbon through it. Put the card in the holder and, if you wish, add some notepaper. Give the gift to your mother on Mother's Day.

Chapter 4: I Can Touch

Song

Same tune as Chapter 1, using the words:
"I've two hands so I can feel."

Craft

Collage (page 13)

Make a collage by gluing on materials of various shapes, sizes, and textures. Use felt, foil, yarn, paper scraps, wallpaper, or foam pieces.

Chapter 5: I Can Taste

Song

Same tune as Chapter 1, using the words:
"I've a mouth so I can taste."

Craft

Pizza (page 17)

Cut out the four pieces of the card. Mix the pieces up and then arrange them in the order that pizza is made.

14

3

Chapter 6: I Can Help

Song

Head, Shoulders, Knees and Toes

Head, shoulders, knees and toes, knees and toes.

Head, shoulders, knees and toes, knees and toes and —

eyes and ears and mouth and nose.

Head, shoulders, knees and toes, knees and toes.

Head, shoulders, knees and toes, knees and toes.   [Touch hands to respective parts.]

Head, shoulders, knees and toes, knees and toes   [Touch hands to respective parts.]

and eyes and ears and mouth and nose.   [Point to respective parts.]

Head, shoulders, knees and toes, knees and toes.   [Touch hands to respective parts.]

Craft
Medal (page 23)
Cut out the medal and write your name on the line. Then punch a hole at the top and string the medal on a piece of ribbon.

Chapter 7: I Can Care

Poem

I'm glad the sky is painted blue
And the earth is painted green,
With such a lot of nice fresh air
All sandwiched in between.

Craft
Jack-in-the-Box (perforated Card B)
Separate the strip. Fold the large section and make a slit in the middle. Decorate the front of the box. Insert Jack in the slit and move him up and down.

Finger Play
God Loves Me

God loves me.	[Clap, clap, point to self.]
And I love you.	[Clap, clap, point forward.]
We show love	[Clap, clap, fold hands over heart.]
By what we do.	[Clap, clap, hold out hands.]

Mary Kathleen Glavich, S.N.D.

Special Lesson 5: Easter

Finger Play
Baby Chick

A baby chick came out of an egg—	[Make a fist and break through
Its beak, its head, a wing, then a leg.	it with the other hand.]
It greeted me with a "peep, peep, peep."	
Then nodded its head and went	[Fold hands at side of head.]
to sleep.	

Mary Kathleen Glavich, S.N.D.

Song
To the tune of "Mary Had a Little Lamb":
1. I can run for I have life,
   I have life, I have life.
   I can run for I have life.
   Thank you, God, for life.
2. I can hop . . .
3. I can spin . . .
4. I can wave . . .
5. I can jump . . .

Craft
Butterfly (perforated Card L)
Punch out the perforated butterfly and punch holes around the wings. Color the butterfly. Harden the ends of a 30-inch piece of ribbon or yarn by dipping them in glue or wrapping them with tape. Starting at the top, lace the ribbon or yarn through the holes. Tie the ribbon or yarn in a bow at the top.

Special Lesson 6: Pentecost

Craft
Paper fan (pages 107–108)
Decorate and fold the paper fan.

4

13

Special Lesson 2: Advent

Song

Love Is Like a Ring

Love is like a ring. ___ A ring that has ___ no end - ing.

2. God loves you and me. God loves us now and always.

Craft

Advent Wreath (perforated Card K)

Punch out the perforated wreath and punch a hole in the top so it can be hung. Glue green macaroni or squares of green paper on the wreath. Glue or staple a red bow on the wreath. String ribbon or yarn through the hole and tie it so that the wreath can be hung.

Special Lesson 3: Christmas

Poem

Christmas Bells

Ring the bells on Christmas morn.
Tell the news that Jesus is born.
Ring them far. Ring them near.
Ring them loud for all to hear.
Over the world let them sing,
Ding, dong, ding, dong, ding, dong, ding.

Mary Kathleen Glavich, S.N.D.

Craft

Christmas Card (page 99)

Color the picture. Put stars in the sky with stickers, crayons, markers, or glitter. Fold the card in half and sign it.

Special Lesson 4: Lent

Finger Play

This is my garden.	[Extend hand, palm up.]
I'll rake it with care.	[Make pulling motion with hands.]
And plant some flower seeds	[Make planting motions with
Right in there.	thumb and index finger.]
The sun will shine,	[Make circle with arms above head.]
The rain will fall.	[Flutter fingers downward.]
And my garden will blossom	[Cup hands;
And grow straight and tall.	raise them slowly.]

Chapter 8: I Can Clean

Craft

Toy Puzzle (perforated Card C)

Separate the pieces, mix them, and then put the puzzle together.

Chapter 9: I Can Share

Craft

A Shared Gift (page 31)

Drop tempera paint on only one side of the line. Then fold over the empty side of the paper onto the paint and press down so that the paint is "shared" with the empty half. Give the card to someone as a gift.

Chapter 10: I Can Smile

Craft

Smiling Face (page 35)

Draw a picture of your happy face in the circle, using crayons or markers. Display your picture so your family can see it.

Chapter 11: I Can Talk

Craft

Megaphone (perforated Card D)

Punch out the megaphone and write your name on it. Decorate it and staple the ends together.

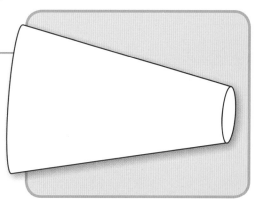

Chapter 12: I Can Pray

Song

Craft

Prayer Book/Doorknob Hanger (perforated Card E)
Separate the two parts. Place your hands on the card with your fingers together and with the dotted line between your thumbs. Have someone trace your hands. (Or make handprints using tempera paint-soaked paper towels as an ink pad.) On the other side of the card draw or glue pictures of things for which you are thankful. Fold the card along the dotted line to form praying hands.

Punch out the circle on the doorknob hanger. Color the sun or glue a yellow felt disk in the circle. Add glitter to the stars. Hang the prayer reminder on a doorknob or wall.

Chapter 13: I Can Sing

Song

Glory to God in the highest!   [Sing on one note.]

Craft

Singing Angel (page 43)
Decorate the angel's robe. Glue glitter on the robe and cotton on the clouds. Fold back the sides of the card so that the angel stands.

Chapter 14: I Can Laugh

Craft

Laughing Child (page 47)
Complete the picture. Add details, such as eyelashes, stripes or flowers on the shirt, socks, and then color the child in. Staple the sides of the card to form a long tube. Glue or staple yarn or ribbon along the top as hair.

Chapter 25: I Can Love

Finger Play

God loves me,	[Clap, clap, point to self.]
And I love you.	[Clap, clap, point forwards.]
We show love	[Clap, clap, fold hands over heart.]
By what we do.	[Clap, clap, hold out hands.]

Mary Kathleen Glavich, S.N.D.

Craft

Love Pocket (page 91)
Cut out the pocket and the three hearts. Color the hearts on the pocket red and glue pieces of paper doilies on or around the bigger heart. Put glue on the green edges of the pocket and fold up the bottom flap. Fold down the top flap.

Special Lesson 1: Halloween/Feast of All Saints

Song

To the tune of "The Farmer in the Dell":
We're friends of Jesus Christ.
We're friends of Jesus Christ.
Heigh-ho the derry-o.
We're friends of Jesus Christ.
2. We try to be like him . . .
3. Someday we'll be with him . . .

Mary Kathleen Glavich, S.N.D.

Craft

Lantern (perforated Card J)
Separate the green strip and fold the card in half lengthwise. Pull apart the perforated lines to make slits in the middle of the card, being careful not to tear the slits to the end of the card. Glue the ends of the lantern together. Glue on the green strip as a handle. Put the lantern out on Halloween night.

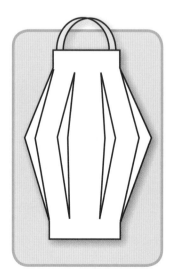

Chapter 23: I Can Learn

Poem

One potato, two potato, three potato, four,
Five potato, six potato, seven potato, more.

Song

Craft

Circle (page 85)

Cut out the circle and write your name on it. Cut along the line on the front to make a spiral, which can be hung.

Chapter 24: I Can Pretend

Craft

Lion (perforated Card I)

Punch out the perforated lion head. Color the eyes and nose black. Fold two pipe cleaners in half and glue them on for whiskers (or draw lines). Glue on strands of yarn for a mane. You might punch at least nine holes around the head and loop an 8-inch piece of yarn in each hole. To loop the yarn, fold a piece of yarn in half and insert the fold into the hole. Open the folded yarn to make a circle and put the tails from the other side through it. Pull the tails to make a knot.

Chapter 15: I Can Celebrate

Finger Play

God is here with us today,
So we say "Hip, hip, hooray!"   [Raise arm three times on "Hip, hip, hooray."]

Craft

Party Hat (perforated Card F)

Punch out the hat and write your name on it. Decorate it with anything green. Staple the hat together. Punch holes where the dots are and tie pieces of yarn on the hat. If you wish, staple green crepe-paper streamers to the top.

Chapter 16: I Can Move

Craft

Tambourine (perforated Card G)

Punch out the tambourine and decorate it. If you wish, staple ribbons or crepe-paper streamers to the circle.
Dance with the tambourine.

Chapter 17: I Can Play

Finger Play

Playful Kittens

Five little kittens
Like to run and play.   [Move fingers on left hand.]
Five other kittens
Are not far away.   [Wiggle fingers on right hand.]

Ten little kittens meet,   [Move both hands in front of chest.]
Having loads of fun.   [Keep moving fingers.]
Along comes a dog.
See those kittens run!   [Move arms outward, fingers moving faster.]

Ten little kittens
Scamper up a tree.   [Move arms over head, fingers moving.]
Ten little kittens said,
"You can't catch me!"
Helen Kitchell Evans

Craft

Squirrel (page 57)

Cut out the tail. Staple the squirrel closed along the side and top to form a hand puppet. Then staple on the tail. (To avoid injury, make sure all staples are closed.) Fold the squirrel's head along the line.

Chapter 18: I Can Work

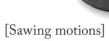

Song

To the tune of "Did You Ever See a Lassie?":

1. Did you ever see a carpenter,
   carpenter, carpenter?
   Did you ever see a carpenter saw   [Sawing motions]
   wood like this?
   We saw wood and saw wood and
   saw wood and saw wood.
   Did you ever see a carpenter saw
   wood like this?
2. . . . pound nails . . .   [Pounding motions]
3. . . . sand wood . . .   [Sanding motions]
4. . . . paint wood . . .   [Painting motions]

Craft

Framed Picture (page 63)

Make designs or a flower in the frame by gluing on cereal, seeds, rice, colored macaroni, or one-inch squares of colored tissue paper.

Chapter 19: I Can Make Things

Finger Play

What God Made

God made the sun and the great blue sky.	[Make a circle with arms; separate arms and raise hands.]
God made the stars and the moon.	[Open and close fingers.]
God made lakes and birds that fly.	[Flap arms.]
God made the little raccoon.	[Make circles with fingers around eyes.]
God made mountains and green, grassy hills.	[Make a peak with hands.]
God made the fish in the sea.	[Put palms together and wiggle hands forward.]
God made flowers like daffodils.	[Pretend to smell flower.]
But best of all, God made me!	[Point to self.]

Mary Kathleen Glavich, S.N.D.

Craft

Dog (perforated Card H)

Punch out the parts of the perforated card. Fold the card so the dog stands. Glue on the head and tail. Name your dog and write it on the dog tag.

Chapter 20: I Can Grow

Finger Play

When I was a baby I was very, very small.	[Stoop down and be as small as possible.]
Today I am just this size.	[Stand and raise hand to top of head.]
And someday I'll be tall.	[Stretch hands high.]

Mary Kathleen Glavich, S.N.D.

Craft

Growth Chart (page 71)

Fold the card. On the cover glue a baby picture, draw a picture of yourself, or put a handprint using tempera paint-soaked paper towels. Fill in the chart from time to time.

Chapter 21: I Can Feel

Craft

Feelings Lamb (page 75)

Color the lamb's eyes on each side of the card. Make a smile on the side without a mouth and draw in tears on the other side. Punch a hole in the top and string yarn or ribbon through it. Hang the lamb on a doorknob and turn the card to match your feelings during the day.

Chapter 22: I Can Wish

Craft

Best Wishes Card (page 81)

Fold the card and write your name on it. Color or paint a design on the front of the card. Give the card to someone special.

Art Credits

The stapler, glue bottle, and scissors icons throughout this book were illustrated by Kathryn Seckman Kirsch.

UNIT 1

3 Phyllis Pollema–Cahill
4 (tl) iStockphoto.com/Emrah Turudu
4 (br) Anika Salsera
4 (ears) William Wise
5 Claudine Gévry
6 Dennis Hockerman
8 Ginna Hirtenstein
9 William Wise
11 Claudine Gévry
12 (tl) Jupiter Images

UNIT 2

21–22 Ginna Hirtenstein
23 iStockphoto.com/Guillermo Lobo
24 Phyllis Pollema–Cahill
25 Nan Brooks
26 (book stack) iStockphoto.com/Julie Deshaies
26 (blue thongs) iStockphoto.com/Anne Clark
28 (green towels) iStockphoto.com/Dawn Liljenquist
29 Nan Brooks
30 Nan Brooks

UNIT 3

37 iStockphoto.com/Ekaterina Monakhova
38 Phil Martin Photography
40 Len Ebert
41 Ginna Hirtenstein
42 Ginna Hirtenstein
43 Len Ebert
45 Nan Brooks
46 (photo) iStockphoto.com/Justin Horrocks
46 (illustrations) Dora Leder
47 Kathryn Seckman Kirsch
49 Claudine Gévry
50 iStockphoto.com/Anant Dummai
51–52 Ethel Gold

UNIT 4

54 William Wise
55 Claudine Gévry
56 Len Ebert
57–58 Kristin Goeters
60 Yoshi Miyake
61–62 Dennis Hockerman
65 Claudine Gévry
66 William Wise
67 iStockphoto.com/Karen Roach
68 (bottle) iStockphoto.com/Christine Balderas
68 (bed) iStockphoto.com/Mykola Velychko
68 (chair) iStockphoto.com/Simon Krzic
69–70 Ginna Hirtenstein
72 Kristin Goeters

UNIT 5

73 Nan Brooks
74 Nan Brooks
75–76 Kristin Goeters
78 (illustrations) Nan Brooks
79–80 Dennis Hockerman
83 iStockphoto.com/Rosemarie Gearhart
84 Meg Elliott Smith
87 iStockphoto.com/Marzanna Syncerz
88 Ethel Gold
90 (tl) iStockphoto.com/Nicole S. Young
90 (bl) Jupiter Images
90 (br) iStockphoto.com/Franky De Meyer

SPECIAL LESSONS

93 Peter Dazeley/Getty Images
94 Yoshi Miyake
95 Ginna Hirtenstein
96 Ginna Hirtenstein
97 Phil Martin Photography
99 Yoshi Miyake
101 (hands) Phil Martin Photography

Continued on next page. ▶

Art Credits

Continued from previous page.

101 (grass) iStockphoto.com/Helle Bro
102 (tl) Jupiter Images
103 Dora Leder
104 iStockphoto.com/Yiying Lu
105 iStockphoto.com/Debi Bishop
106 (tr) iStockphoto.com/John Said
106 (bl) Jupiter Images
106 (br) iStockphoto.com/Slawomir Jastrzebski
109 (tl) iStockphoto.com/Nikolay Suslov
109 (tr) iStockphoto.com/Mikael Damkier
110 Len Ebert
111 Meg Elliott Smith
112 iStockphoto.com/Bill Noll
113 Phyllis Pollema–Cahill
114 Meg Elliott Smith
117 Phyllis Pollema–Cahill
118 (mother) iStockphoto.com/Justin Horrocks
118 (horses) iStockphoto.com/Eric Isselée
121 iStockphoto.com/Marzanna Syncerz
122 Claudine Gévry
126 Meg Elliott Smith
129 iStockphoto.com/Ron Chapple
130 (sun) iStockphoto.com/Lucíade Salterain
131 Susan Tolonen

FAMILY ACTIVITY BOOKLET

133 (tc,tr) Jupiter Images
133 (bl) iStockphoto.com/Achim Prill
133 (br) iStockphoto.com/Katuya Shima
134 (l) iStockphoto.com/Alexander Hafemann
134 (tr) iStockphoto.com/Danny Hooks
134 (br) Jupiter Images

135 (tl,bl) Meg Elliott Smith
135 (tr) iStockphoto.com/Sean Locke
135 (br) iStockphoto.com/David Hernandez
136 (bl) Meg Elliott Smith
136 (tr) iStockphoto.com/Nicole S. Young
136 (br) iStockphoto.com/Wojtek Kryczka
137 (bl) iStockphoto.com/Ivan Mateev
137 (br) Meg Elliott Smith
138 (tl) iStockphoto.com/Derek Thomas
138 (tr,br) Meg Elliott Smith
139 (bl,br) Meg Elliott Smith
140 (br) Jupiter Images

ART CREDITS

141–142 (paint drips) iStockphoto.com/Slavoljub Pantelic

PERFORATED CARDS

A (window, curtains) iStockphoto.com/Jolande Gerritsen
B Juan Castillo
C Juan Castillo
E (sun, moon, stars) iStockphoto.com/Prohor Gabrusenoc
G (bells) Jupiter Images
G (musical notes) iStockphoto.com/Maria Ahlfors
H (dog tag) Jupiter Images
H (illustration) Kristin Goeters
I Kristin Goeters
L (butterfly) William Wise

Photos and illustrations not acknowledged above are either owned by Loyola Press or from royalty–free sources including, but not limited to Agnus, Alamy, Comstock, Corbis, Creatas, Fotosearch, Getty Images, Imagestate, iStock, Jupiter Images, Punchstock, Rubberball, and Veer. Loyola Press has made every effort to locate the copyright holders for the cited works used in this publication and to make full acknowledgment for their use. In the case of any omissions, the Publisher will be pleased to make suitable acknowledgments in future editions.

Perforated Cards

© LOYOLAPRESS.

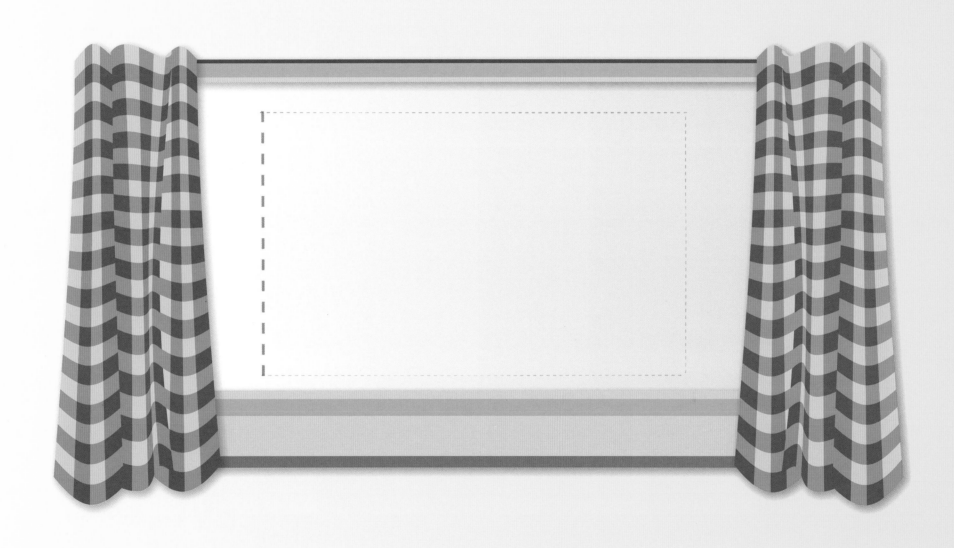

© LOYOLAPRESS.

© LOYOLAPRESS.

Name _____

© LOYOLA PRESS.

Name

© LOYOLA PRESS.

I love you.

Name _____

Name _____

© LOYOLA PRESS.

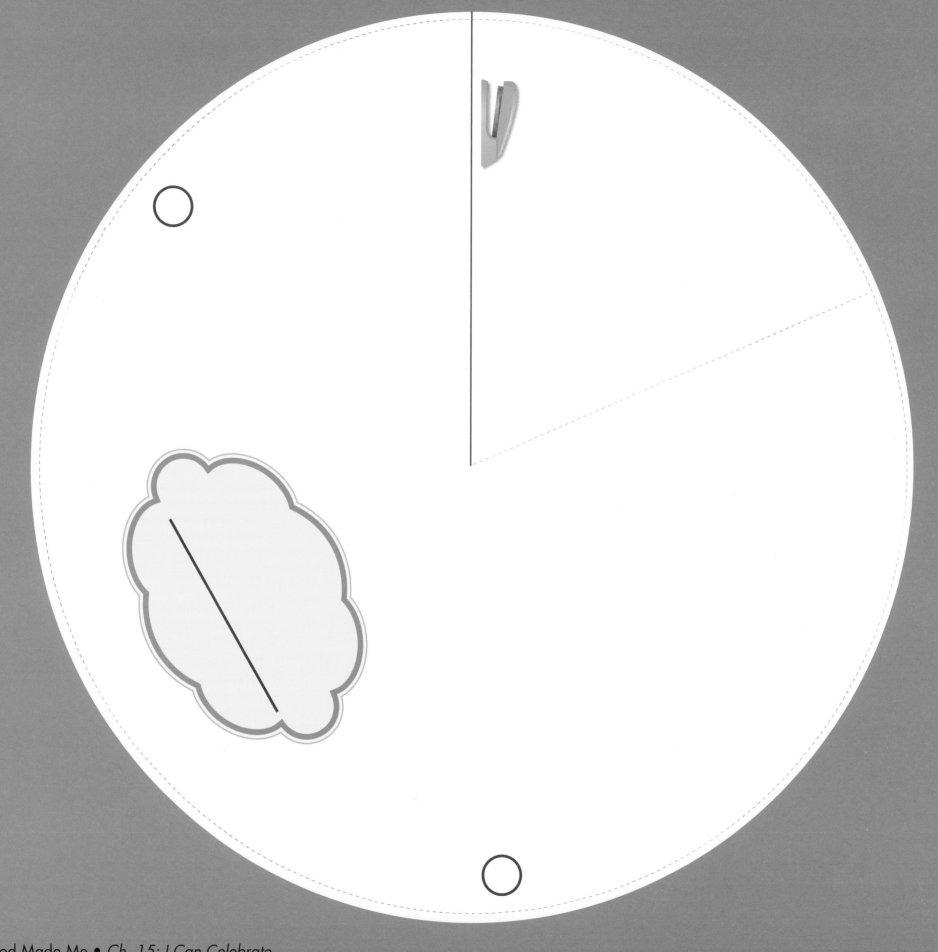

© LOYOLAPRESS.

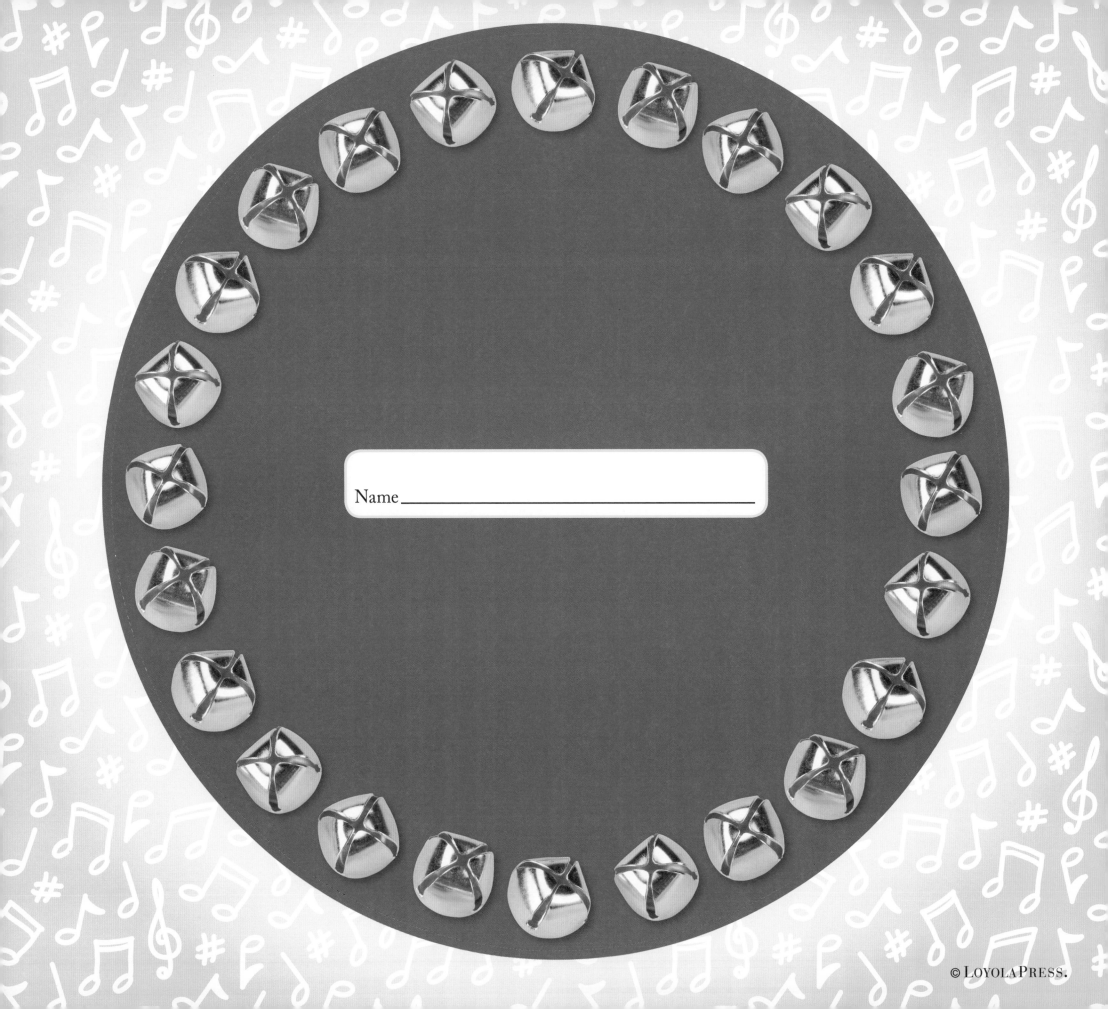

Name _____

© LOYOLAPRESS.

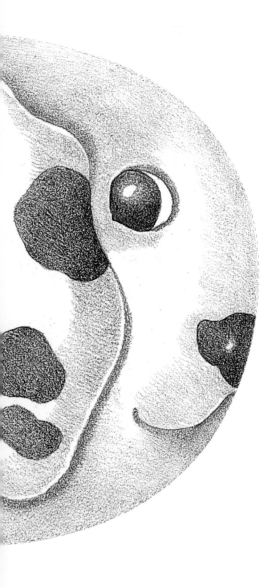

Tail

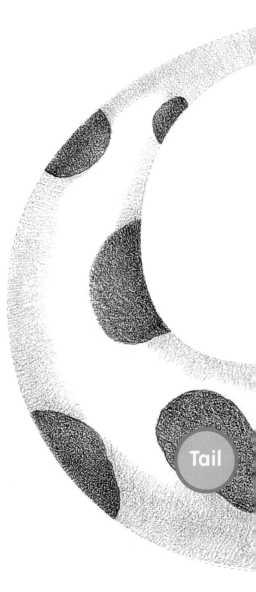

Tail

Name _____

© LOYOLA PRESS.

My name is:

_____

My lion friend's name is:

_____

© LOYOLAPRESS.

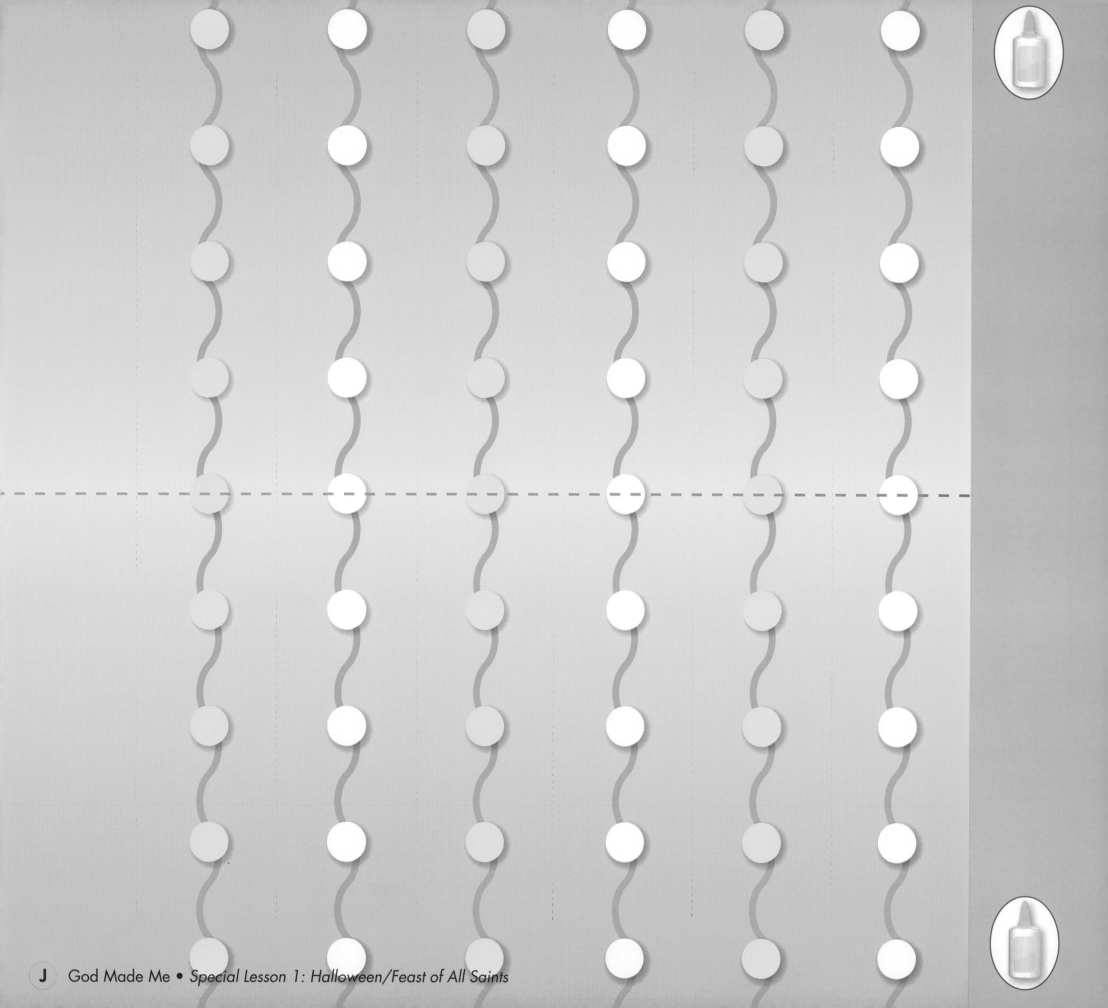

Name _____

© LOYOLA PRESS.

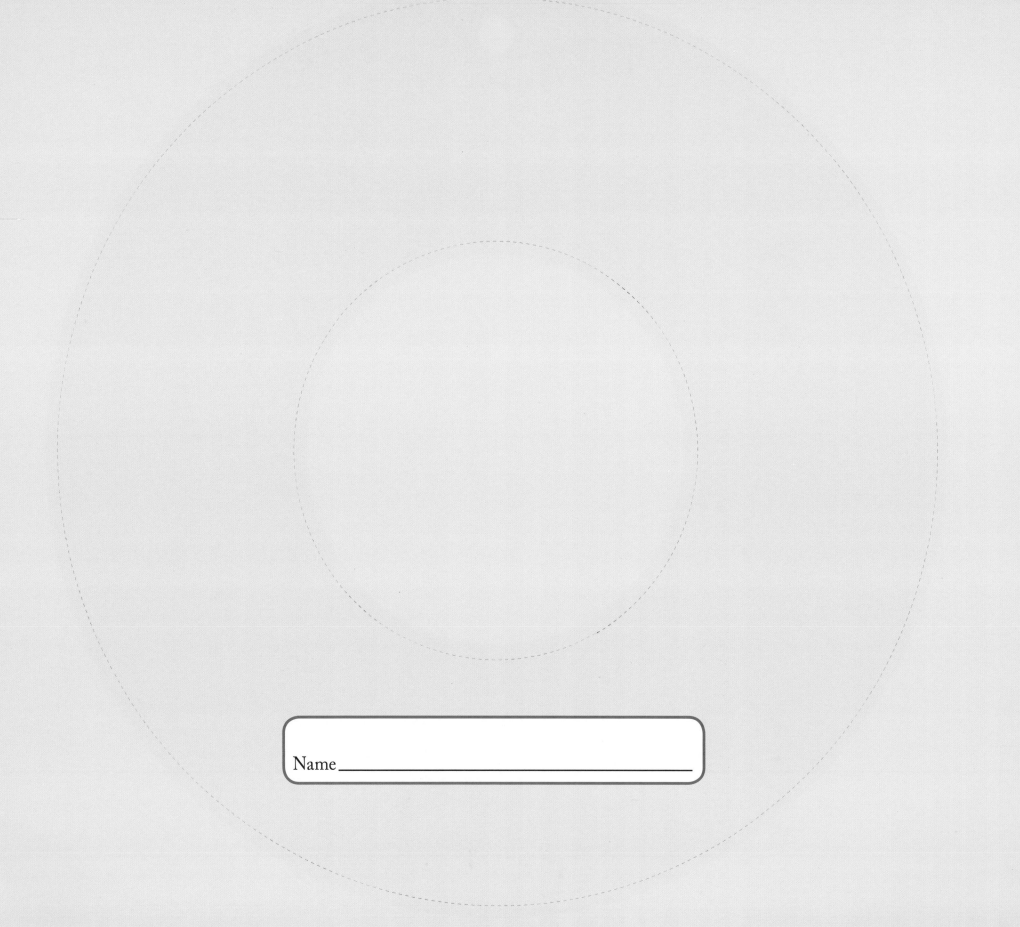

Name _____

© LOYOLAPRESS.

Name _____

© LOYOLAPRESS.